3·00

1st edition, 1971.

THE POULTRY AND GAME COOKBOOK

Books by Ruth Martin

MODERN PARTY COOKING
EASY TO COOK
MAKE ME AN EXPERT MEAT COOK

The Poultry
and
Game Cookbook

compiled
by

Ruth Martin

Decorations by Gillian Kenny

ANGUS AND ROBERTSON

ANGUS & ROBERTSON (PUBLISHERS) PTY LTD
54 Bartholomew Close, London
221 George Street, Sydney
107 Elizabeth Street, Melbourne
89 Anson Road, Singapore

© 1971 by Ruth Martin

ISBN 0 207 95426 7

First published in the United Kingdom in 1971

Printed in Great Britain by
MORRISON AND GIBB LTD, LONDON AND EDINBURGH

Contents

Introduction

The enormous growth of the poultry industry in recent times has been reflected even in the humblest kitchen. In countless homes, chicken—and even more so, turkey—once made an appearance only at Christmas-time or on very special family occasions. Now they feature frequently on the housewife's shopping list and represent good value for money. Even ducks, which were rarely seen in shops except at Christmas, are now available all the time and, since they are rather less economical, have taken over the more glamorous role that chicken once had.

The marketing of chicken halves and portions has been so hugely successful that it is now being extended to turkey, and this opens up a whole new range of possibilities for the variety-seeking cook.

However, far too many people still limit their poultry cooking to the straightforward "roast", and it is a sad fact that the palate tires much more quickly of roast poultry than it does of roast meats. The object of this book is to show that there is an infinite variety in the ways that birds can be served—hot or cold, some very simple, others more ambitious. In addition to roasting-with-a-difference recipes, there are world-ranging ideas for using whole, half- or quarter-birds, as well as the packets of breasts and drumsticks now available. You will find, too, plenty of ways to make exciting dishes out of the rather boring remains of a large cold bird.

Country-dwellers perhaps have more access to game birds than town folk, but pheasant, partridge, pigeon and so on are frequently to be found in poulterers' shops. The treatment and preparation of game birds are, therefore, included in this book, together with suggestions as to the form in which they can be brought to the table.

Soups

Hot Soups

Never throw away the carcase of your poultry, particularly turkey and chicken, without extracting from it the last scrap of value and nutriment. Use the carcase to make stock from which any number of differing soups can be prepared.

BROWN CHICKEN SOUP

1 ounce butter
carcase of bird, etc
giblets
3 or 4 spring onions
1 medium-sized tomato
pinch of basil

a little gravy browning powder, or 1 ounce flour and browning drops
seasoning
water

Place the carcase, bones and giblets in a stewpan. Add the onions (sliced), the tomato (cut in four), the seasoning, any oddments of forcemeat left over, and the basil. Pour over 2 to 2½ pints of water, bring to the boil and simmer for 2 hours. Strain into a basin. If not wanted immediately, leave to cool, then skim off any fat. Otherwise, keep hot. Meanwhile, remove any scraps of flesh from bones and carcase, chop liver and flesh very finely and add to broth. Melt butter in a pan, mix in the gravy browning powder (or the flour and a few drops of liquid browning). When blended and cooked, gradually add the stock, make it piping hot and serve, garnished with fried bread croûtons.

BASIC CHICKEN STOCK

1 carcase
1 onion
2 carrots
1 turnip (small)
salt and pepper

sprigs of parsley
sprigs of thyme
1 bay leaf
4 pints cold water

Using a large saucepan, break the carcase into pieces, add any scraps of left-over meat and stuffing. Peel and rough-cut the vegetables, add the seasoning and pour on the water. In order to extract the maximum

3

flavour, bring the pot slowly to the boil. Simmer until the liquid has reduced by about one-third (about an hour), then strain into a bowl and leave to cool.

If using a pressure cooker, take care to follow the manufacturer's instructions about over-filling. Cooking time at 15 pounds pressure is 20 minutes, and you can reduce the initial water quantity to 3 pints. When the stock is cold, remove any fat from the surface. The stock is then ready for use, but should be reboiled each day unless stored in a refrigerator. The stock should not be kept in any case more than three days because it encourages the development of bacteria which can lead to food poisoning.

BASIC TURKEY STOCK

Substituting your turkey carcase, follow the instructions for Basic Chicken Stock, but increase the quantity of water by half.

These stocks can be used for any soup recipe calling for white stock, or for any of the following.

CHICKEN AND RICE SOUP

2–3 slices streaky bacon	1 parsnip or turnip
1 large carrot	2 celery stalks
1 onion	2 pints chicken stock
1 potato	2 tablespoons Patna rice

Grate the vegetables, chop the celery stalks and fry in oil, together with the bacon slices, chopped. Add the chicken stock, bring to the boil, drop in the rice and simmer for about 25 minutes.

CHICKEN AND CAULIFLOWER CREAM

1 small cauliflower	2 pints chicken stock
1 onion	1 level tablespoon cornflour
salt and pepper	1 small cup milk

Break the cauliflower into small pieces, grate the onion, mix into the stock, season, bring to the boil and simmer for 30 minutes. Strain, pulp the vegetables, and blend together. Mix the cornflour into the milk, stir carefully into the soup and bring back to boiling. Boil 2 minutes, check the flavour, add further seasoning if necessary. Serve with toast or fried croûtons of bread.

MUSHROOM SOUP

2 ounces butter
½ pound sliced mushrooms
1 ounce chopped onions
1½ ounces flour
1 pint chicken stock

¼ pint hot milk
salt and pepper to taste
pinch of nutmeg
chopped parsley

Heat the butter in a pan. Add sliced mushrooms and chopped onions. Allow to cook for a few minutes. Sprinkle in the flour. Stir well, until flour has been absorbed. Allow to cook for a further 2 minutes. Gradually add boiling chicken stock and hot milk. Stir well. Season to taste with salt, pepper and a pinch of nutmeg. Allow to simmer for 15 minutes before serving, sprinkled with parsley.

ONION SOUP AU GRATIN

4 or 5 Spanish onions, skinned
    and sliced or diced
4 dessertspoons butter
1 quart stock or chicken broth

salt and pepper
toasted French bread
grated Parmesan cheese

Sauté onions in butter until lightly browned. Add stock and broth, either to the pan in which you have browned the onions or to a large casserole to which you transfer the onions. Salt and pepper to taste, allow the soup to come to the boil, and simmer 15 minutes.

Serve with slices of well toasted French bread heaped with grated Parmesan cheese and lightly browned under the grill. Serve with additional grated cheese.

Variations

CLEAR ONION SOUP

Strain the soup. Serve with toasted French bread and grated Parmesan cheese.

ONION SOUP WITH WINE

Add ½ cup dry white wine to the broth after adding broth to the onions.

ONION SOUP IN CASSEROLE

Transfer the soup to individual heat-proof dishes. Top each one with a slice of toast and heap with grated cheese. Place in a moderate oven (375° F, Gas 5) for 10 minutes.

WATERCRESS SOUP

4 ounces watercress leaves	1 level dessertspoon chopped
½ tablespoon butter	chervil or parsley
1 small egg yolk	salt and pepper
¼ cup cream	1 pint chicken stock

Wash and dry the watercress, chop roughly and cook it over a low flame in the melted butter for 5 minutes. Stir in the stock and seasoning and simmer for 30 minutes.

Blend the egg yolk into the cream, stir in the herb and add to the soup. Heat through but do not allow the soup to boil. Serve with bread croûtons.

CHINESE CHICKEN SOUP

2 pints chicken broth	1 ounce bamboo shoots
4 pieces dried mushrooms	salt
1 chicken breast	

Finely slice the chicken breast, bamboo shoots and mushrooms. Bring the broth to the boil, drop in the shredded ingredients, season with salt to taste. Cook gently for 3 to 5 minutes. Serve in small individual bowls.

CHINESE CORN AND CHICKEN SOUP

1 large tin creamed sweet-corn	3½ cups water
3 eggs	2 tablespoons cornflour
1 slice cooked ham	1 tablespoon sherry
3 cups chicken broth	2 tablespoons salt

Mix the cornflour in half a cup of water. Put the remaining water together with the stock, salt and sherry, in a large pan and bring to the boil. Add the sweet-corn, reboil and cook 4 minutes. Reduce the heat to low, dribble in the beaten eggs to form "flowers". Now stir in the cornflour-water mixture, stir, and continue cooking and stirring for 2 minutes after the soup has thickened. Serve with the cooked ham (chopped) for garnish.

FRENCH GREEN PEA AND CHICKEN SOUP

5 cups fresh peas	2 teaspoons sugar
6 dessertspoons butter	½ teaspoon salt
1 onion	1¼ cups water

1 young lettuce

spinach

parsley

chervil (optional)

chicken stock

$\frac{1}{4}$ cup cooked white chicken meat

3 egg yolks

1$\frac{1}{2}$ cups single cream

In a large saucepan put 4 cups of fresh peas, the butter, the finely minced onion, the lettuce cut in julienne strips, about 15 leaves of fresh spinach, a sprig of parsley, a few sprigs of chervil if you have it, the sugar, salt, and water. Cover the saucepan, bring the soup to the boil, and cook it over a moderate heat until the peas are tender. Meanwhile, boil 1 cup of fresh peas, in a separate pan, to add to the soup later. Strain the soup, pressing the vegetables through with the liquid or mix in a blender. Return the soup to the saucepan, add 3 cups of chicken stock, stir well, and simmer over a low heat for about 15 minutes. Then add the extra cup of peas, drained, and the chicken meat cut into very fine julienne strips. Mix the egg yolks with the cream, and add this gradually to the soup, stirring constantly. Continue cooking until the soup thickens to a creamy consistency, but do not let it boil. This makes a large quantity, sufficient for about 8 servings.

TURKEY SOUP

1 turkey carcase

stock or water to cover

1 onion

salt and pepper

bouquet garni

little Worcester sauce

squeeze of orange or lemon juice

little sherry

sprig of parsley

Remove any stuffing from the carcase and reserve a little meat. Cut this into dice as a garnish. Break up bones, put into a large saucepan and cover with stock or water, allowing $\frac{1}{4}$ pint for each portion. Peel and slice onion. Add to pan with a little salt and pepper, bouquet garni, a dash of Worcester sauce and orange or lemon juice. Bring to the boil, then reduce heat, cover and simmer for 2 to 3 hours, skimming occasionally. Strain and allow to cool. When cold, remove all fat from surface and reheat, adding diced meat and sherry.

TURKEY NOODLE SOUP

turkey carcase

1 large onion

4 cloves

1 large carrot

2 stalks celery, with leaves

6 peppercorns

bouquet garni (sprig of parsley,

       thyme and small bay leaf)

salt, to taste

1 teacup noodles

Remove any remaining meat from the carcase. Cut meat into small pieces and reserve. Crack bones and place with all remaining ingredients, except the noodles, in a large saucepan. Cover with at least 2½ pints cold water. Bring slowly to the boil. Half cover the pan and simmer very slowly for 3 to 4 hours. Strain and chill the stock. Then skim off any fat from the top. Before serving, add any reserved meat to the stock, bring it quickly to the boil and simmer for 15 minutes. Meanwhile cook the noodles until tender in a quart of boiling, salted water, then drain. Add hot, drained noodles to the soup, and serve.

GIBLET SOUP

1 set turkey or goose giblets	1 teaspoon salt
2 pints water	5 peppercorns
1 celery stalk	parsley (2 sprigs)
1 carrot	thyme (2 sprigs)
1 onion	1 ounce flour
1 clove	1 ounce margarine

Wash and trim the giblets, cover with water and bring slowly to simmering. Add the vegetables, herbs, spices and seasoning and simmer for at least 2 hours. Strain. Melt the margarine in a saucepan, stir in the flour and cook until it browns—take care not to burn. Gradually stir in the stock, bring back to the boil and cook, stirring, for about 5 minutes. Add the best of the giblet flesh, diced very small. Taste for seasoning and adjust as necessary. (You can make this with chicken giblets, but you will need at least 2 sets for this quantity of water, etc.)

GAME SOUP

2 partridge carcases and trimmings (or equivalent in other game birds)	1 carrot
	2 pints stock
	bouquet garni of parsley, thyme and bay leaf
2 rashers lean bacon	1 tablespoon margarine
1 or 2 slices breast of bird	salt and pepper
1 celery stalk	½ ounce flour
1 onion	

Melt the margarine in a large saucepan and in it brown the carcases and bird trimmings and fry the bacon. Remove them while you fry the vegetables, roughly diced. Stir in the flour and cook till golden, then add the stock and bring to the boil. Put back the birds and bacon, add herbs and seasoning and simmer for about 2 hours. Strain, add to the liquid the bird breast, diced very small, and reheat, checking the flavour for seasoning.

CARROT AND POTATO SOUP

1½ pounds potatoes	2 pints stock
1 pound sliced carrots	salt and pepper
1 small sliced onion or shallot	a little grated nutmeg
3 ounces butter	chopped parsley
1 teaspoon sugar	4 tablespoons thick cream

Peel the potatoes thinly, and cut into slices or dice roughly. Melt half the butter in a saucepan, add the onion, and cook until softened but not brown. Add potatoes and carrots, stir well, add sugar and a little salt. When the vegetables have absorbed the butter, add the stock and cook until vegetables are tender. Rub through a sieve, or put into a liquidizer. Return to the saucepan. Reheat, adjust the seasoning, add a dash of nutmeg and a little more stock if soup is too thick. Just before serving, add remaining butter and cream, and stir in a little freshly chopped parsley.

PARMENTIER SOUP

1 pound potatoes	4 tablespoons milk
2 to 3 leeks (white part only)	3 tablespoons cream
2 ounces butter	salt and pepper
1 pint stock	chopped parsley, chives or chervil

Peel the potatoes thinly, and cut into thick slices. Clean the leeks, cut into pieces and sauté in half the butter, taking care not to brown them. Add potatoes, stock, and salt. Cook until the vegetables are soft. Rub through a sieve, or put into a liquidizer. Return to the saucepan, adjust the seasoning, and reheat. Just before serving, stir in the rest of the butter, milk and cream. Sprinkle with freshly chopped parsley, and serve hot or cold.

POTATO AND WATERCRESS SOUP

1 pound potatoes	¼ pint milk
1 large sliced onion	salt and pepper
1 bunch chopped watercress	a little grated nutmeg
1 pint stock	

Peel the potatoes thinly, and cook with the onion in the stock until tender. Rub through a sieve, or put into a liquidizer. Return to the saucepan, add the milk, and reheat. Adjust the seasoning, add a dash of grated nutmeg and, before serving, stir in the chopped watercress.

POTATO AND CELERY SOUP

1 pound potatoes	$\frac{1}{4}$ pint milk
$\frac{1}{2}$ head celery	salt and pepper
2 onions	chopped parsley
1 ounce butter	grated Cheddar cheese if liked
1 pint stock	

Separate the sticks of celery, wash thoroughly and cut into pieces. Peel the potatoes thinly and cut into quarters. Peel and slice the onions. Melt the butter in a saucepan, add the celery and onion, and cook gently without browning. Add the potatoes, stock, and seasoning. Bring to the boil, and simmer gently until the vegetables are cooked. Rub through a sieve, or put into a liquidizer. Add the milk, reheat, and adjust the seasoning. Serve piping hot, sprinkled with freshly chopped parsley or grated cheese.

Cold Soups

Cold soup on a hot day is as appetizing as a hot soup is on a cold day. All of the last three soups mentioned above are delicious and refreshing when served iced in summer weather. Another favourite summer soup is Vichysoisse, although this can be served hot if preferred.

VICHYSOISSE

2 tablespoons butter	2 tablespoons top of milk
2 leeks	1 pint chicken stock
$\frac{1}{2}$ onion	Worcester sauce
1 stalk celery	pinch nutmeg
1 potato	chopped chives
salt and pepper	

Melt the butter, add the finely chopped leeks and onion. Cook slowly until transparent, then add chopped celery, sliced potato, salt, pepper and stock. Cook until all vegetables are tender, add other seasonings to taste. Put through a sieve, and add the milk (also more stock if needed to make up quantity to 1½ pints). Serve chilled, with sprinkling of chopped chives.

ICED CUCUMBER SOUP

1 large cucumber	1 ounce butter or good quality
1 large onion	margarine
1 pint stock	salt and pepper
½ pint milk	1 lemon

Slice the onion thinly and fry in the fat till tender. Add the stock and the cucumber, partially peeled and cut into small chunks. Season to taste, and simmer for 25 minutes. Remove from heat, pass the mixture through a sieve and allow to cool. Then add the milk, and freeze the soup lightly in refrigerator. Serve in cold soup bowls topped with thin lemon slices.

Soup from Whole Birds

For a first-class Chicken Broth or for the famous Cock-a-Leekie, you need a whole small boiling fowl.

CHICKEN BROTH

1 small boiling fowl	2 level teaspoons salt
4 pints water	¼ teaspoon pepper
1 carrot	2 celery stalks or a bunch of
1 onion	herbs (thyme, parsley,
1 bay leaf	marjoram)
1 blade mace	1 tablespoon Patna rice
piece of lemon rind	1 tablespoon chopped parsley

Wash and joint the bird, put in a large pan with the water and giblets, seasoning and vegetables, bring slowly to the boil and simmer for 3 to

4 hours, adding more water if needed. Strain the broth through a colander, return it to the pan, skimming off as much fat as possible with a metal spoon. Sprinkle in the rice, bring back to the boil and simmer for 20 minutes. Serve, sprinkled with the chopped parsley.

The chicken meat may be served as a separate dish, or used for a fricassée or other recipe requiring chicken flesh. You may, of course, chop some of the meat finely and add it to the broth.

Variation

TO MAKE A THICK CHICKEN SOUP

2 pints chicken broth (as above)
4 ounces cooked flesh
1 ounce butter

1 ounce flour
4 tablespoons milk
a little nutmeg

Blend the chicken meat in an electric blender or pass through a sieve. Melt the butter, stir in the flour, add stock slowly, heat till boiling. Cook for 2 minutes, then gradually add puréed chicken meat. Add salt and pepper if required and a dash of nutmeg. Finally add the milk, reheat but do not allow to boil.

COCK-A-LEEKIE

1 small boiling fowl
4 ounces prunes
1 pound leeks

2 teaspoons salt
pepper
water to cover

Soak the prunes overnight. Clean the fowl, wash the giblets, place in a large saucepan and cover with water. Bring slowly to simmering point, add salt and pepper, and simmer for 1 hour. Then add the leeks, cleaned and sliced, and simmer for a further 2 hours. Finally add the prunes, stoned and halved, and simmer again for 30 minutes. Serve the chicken meat in the soup or as a main course.

BELGIAN CHICKEN SOUP

1 chicken
2 carrots
3 leeks
4 sticks celery
2 onions
1 lemon

½ ounce butter
parsley, thyme and a bay leaf
salt and pepper
½ bottle dry white wine
1 pint chicken stock

Slice the carrots and cook them gently in the butter. Shred the celery, leeks and onions very finely. Rub the chicken all over with the lemon, and place in a deep saucepan or a large casserole. Pour over it the chicken stock, then add the vegetables, herbs and seasoning. Bring to the boil. Next, add the wine. Cover closely, bring up to boiling point again, then reduce the heat immediately and simmer on a low flame or in a slow oven until the bird is tender. This will depend on the age and size of the bird, but the use of a roasting bird is preferable.

When ready, take up the chicken and carve it. Lay in a deep serving dish, pour the stock over the carved bird and garnish with the vegetables, a little finely chopped parsley, and some croûtons of fried bread.

Additions to Soups

As you can see, the preceding soups made from whole birds can form substantial one-dish meals of liquid and solids. Served with crusty bread, they are very satisfying repasts. Some of the earlier soup recipes in this section, such as Turkey Noodle Soup, Chinese Corn and Chicken Soup and the French Green Pea and Chicken Soup make a meal in themselves for lunch or supper. But any liquid soup can be given extra bulk by the addition of noodles, spaghetti or other pasta, or easily-made dumplings.

SEMOLINA DUMPLINGS

2 eggs
1 dessertspoon butter
$\frac{1}{2}$ pint milk

$\frac{1}{2}$ breakfast cup semolina
salt and pepper

Heat the milk and butter together, gradually stir in the semolina, bring to the boil and cook, stirring, for 5 minutes. Season, and take off the stove. Separate the eggs, beat the yolks briefly and stir into the semolina. Fold the stiffly-whipped whites into the mixture. Have ready a pan of boiling, salted water over a low heat, and drop in the mixture a teaspoonful at a time. In about 7 or 8 minutes the dumplings will rise to the top, indicating that they are cooked. Drain and add to your prepared soup.

CHICKEN LIVER DUMPLINGS

4 chicken livers (uncooked)	1 tablespoon fresh parsley
2 ounces butter	(chopped)
2 ounces flour	salt and pepper
1 slice bread	milk

Chop the livers very finely and mix with the flour, butter (softened), herbs, seasoning and egg. Soak the bread in milk, and add as much of it as is needed to bind the mixture. Beat together very thoroughly, form into small balls, then simmer the dumplings in the soup for 10 to 15 minutes.

POTATO DUMPLINGS

1 pound potatoes	salt and pepper
1 egg	1 tablespoon chopped parsley
4 ounces self-raising flour	1 small grated onion (optional)

Peel the potatoes thinly, and boil in salted water. Drain well, and put through a "ricer" or sieve, or mash well. Add the egg, flour, parsley, seasoning, and onion if liked. Mix well together, and form into small balls, using a little flour to prevent sticking. Place the dumplings in the soup and simmer until the dumplings are cooked, 15 to 30 minutes according to size.

Chicken

In this section you will find information on the preparation and cooking of chickens, fresh or frozen, whole or jointed. First, however, here are some general principles to help you in choosing your bird.

SIZES AND TYPES

Poussins	Smallest and youngest birds on the market, weighing about 1½ pounds and serving one or two people. They are best split down the middle, brushed with melted butter and grilled 10 to 15 minutes per side.
Spring chicken	Birds of 2 to 3 pounds serving two to three people.
Chicken	Birds of 3 to 5 pounds serving up to five people.
Capon	Desexed bird of 6 to 8 pounds serving normally up to 10 people but possibly 12 (see Jointing, p. 20).
Boiling fowl	Older birds, not suitable for roasting but admirable for soup-making or cooking by slow-heat methods.

FRESH BIRDS

Most housewives today buy table-ready birds, but if you have occasion to buy one which is unplucked or, alternatively, plucked but not drawn, here are some points to note.

Feathers should be soft and full, wing quills should come out easily, comb and wattles should be small and there should not be any long hairs.

The skin of a young bird should be white and unwrinkled, the breast-bone pliable and the breast plump. The stiffer the breast-bone and the harder and dryer the feet, the older the bird. Beware of shrunken eyes, soft, flabby feet, or greenish tinge of flesh. Never buy a bird with a "gamey" smell.

FROZEN BIRDS

Only first-quality birds are processed by the manufacturers, so you have no worries on that score. However, it is of the greatest importance that the bird should be *thoroughly thawed* before cooking. This applies equally to chicken joints and all other frozen poultry.

Failure to thaw completely can result in food poisoning. The time required to thaw a whole chicken from solid, at room temperature, is 8 to 12 hours, depending on size. Bacteria are killed during the cooking process. However, if the poultry is incompletely thawed and is then cooked only for the time allowed for wholly soft birds, parts of the meat will be undercooked and it is here that the danger of still-active bacteria lies.

In these days of "oven-ready" poultry, the housewife is not often called upon to practise the arts of plucking, drawing and dressing birds. However, since no poultry and game book would be complete without instructions on these points, they are included here for the benefit of those who may have their own birds, or may be given unprepared birds or, indeed, may wish to buy them in this form from butcher or poulterer.

PLUCKING AND SINGEING

Plucking can be a tedious job unless it is done immediately after the bird is killed and while the body is still warm. Place the bird breast downwards on a large sheet of paper or clean cloth, draw out one wing and commence to pluck the underwing feathers, taking only a very few at a time, so as not to tear the skin. Work towards the breast, then down to the tail, and repeat on the other side. The large flight feathers at the end of the wings will need hard pulling or they can be snapped away from the direction of growth.

Once all the feathers have been removed, some hairs or down may remain and this can be singed away with a lighted taper. Do not, however, singe off any stray feathers because these will give off a strong, unpleasant smell which will permeate the flesh of the bird and spoil it.

If you happen to have the unenviable task of plucking a cold bird, tie its feet together with string and hang over a hook fixed firmly to the wall, then proceed as above.

One time-honoured method of making plucking easier is to plunge the bird very briefly in almost-boiling water. But once the feathers have been removed, make sure that the bird is thoroughly dry before using the lighted taper on hairs and down.

DRAWING

Cut off the head from about two inches down the neck. Turning the bird on to its breast, insert a sharp knife under the skin and slit it down to the base. Loosen the skin, then cut off the neck at the trunk. Throw away the head, but keep the neck to add to the giblets for stockmaking. Slit the skin down just enough to allow you to insert your fingers to loosen the crop and gizzard.

Slip a sharp knife under the leg skin just above the foot, bend and snap the bone, then draw out the tendons, one at a time, by inserting a skewer under them, and, holding firmly on to the foot, drawing them from the flesh. This is a necessary operation, because these tendons, if left in, will make the flesh tough. Detach the feet which can, if you wish, be added to the stock ingredients.

Cut a slit at the vent end of the bird but take care not to pierce the gall bladder and other entrails, as this would give a bitter flavour to the flesh. Insert your fore- and middle fingers and gently loosen the heart and other organs and gradually draw them out. Draw down the crop and gizzard from the neck end. With a clean cloth wrapped round your index finger, take out the lungs by pressing along the ribs, starting at the backbone. When the bird is clean, trim the vent neatly.

Carefully separate the liver from the gall bladder, reserve the neck, gizzard (cleaned of its grit container), liver, heart and—if liked—the feet for making stock, and burn or otherwise dispose of the inedible remains; that is, the head, intestines, lungs, crop and grit from the gizzard.

WIPING OR WASHING
Fresh (non-frozen) birds
It has long been considered that wiping out the cavity with a clean, damp cloth is all that is necessary, and that rinsing the bird through with water destroys a certain amount of its flavour. Some people, however, feel impelled to wash the bird, so in the final analysis this must be a personal choice.

Frozen birds
It is of the utmost importance that frozen birds are thoroughly thawed before cooking (see page 17). Failure to do so can infect the meat and some authorities are now recommending that all frozen birds should be washed before cooking.

STUFFING (see page 21 for suggested stuffings, also individual recipes)
The clean bird may now be stuffed at the neck end and the skin folded over and stitched with needle and cotton to keep it in place. This stitching should, of course, be cut away when the bird is dished up after cooking.

If the bird is large, a different stuffing can also be placed in the body cavity, but the quantity should be limited so that there is plenty of room for the hot air to circulate in the bird during cooking.

Alternatively, stuffing can be baked separately, in a dish, or made into small balls, brushed with oil or melted fat, and cooked for 15 to 25 minutes, depending on the heat of the oven.

TRUSSING
Trussing is done purely for the sake of neat appearance and easier carving. It makes no other difference to the final cooked result whether a bird is trussed or not.

Laying the bird on its back, fold the wing tips back towards the backbone and press the legs well into the side to raise the breast. Thread a trussing needle with clean, fine string and pass the needle through the first wing joint, through the bird and out through the wing joint on the other side. Insert again in the first wing joint, pass again through the body to the first wing joint on the other side. Tie the ends with a bow for easy removal after cooking.

Make a slit in the skin above the vent and push the "parson's nose" through the slit. The legs may simply be tied firmly to the "parson's nose", or another piece of string may first be run through the hock joints and body (twice) under the breast-bone and tied with a bow.

JOINTING

The simplest way of preparing a dish using chicken joints is, of course, to buy the pieces ready cut. If you want to serve more numerous but somewhat smaller pieces, buy generously-sized portions and redivide them at the bone joints, so that you can obtain two servings from each leg joint. You can, of course, also buy packets of drum-sticks and packets of chicken breasts for particular dishes.

TO JOINT A WHOLE BIRD

Lift the legs, one by one, from the body, cut through the skin and press the leg outwards till the joint breaks away from the back-bone. If the bird is small, use whole. Otherwise, redivide at the knuckles with kitchen scissors. Turn the neck of the carcase towards you, cut off the pinions (cook these with the giblets to make gravy) and cut the breast meat straight along the breast-bone to the wing joint. Break the joint and cut it away so that with the breast meat, it is in one piece. Again, this can be redivided to make two portions.

Cut down the back of the carcase from vent to neck end, to provide two more portions.

With a large chicken, it is possible to divide into twelve portions, as follows.

legs —2 portions each	—4 portions
wings—2 portions each	—4 portions
breast—removed whole by cutting through ribs	
with scissors and divided lengthwise	—2 portions
back —divided lengthwise	—2 portions

COOKING THE BIRD
Larding or barding

To overcome the tendency of poultry flesh to dryness, the breast can be either larded or barded. Larding is done by threading a special larding needle with long thin strips of hard fat bacon and threading it through the flesh, leaving the ends protruding.

Barding is covering the breast with rashers of very fat bacon and, if necessary, tying them in place.

Cooking times
Heat the oven at 425° F (Gas 7) and cook the bird at this temperature for the first 20 minutes. Then lower to 375° F (Gas 5) and allow 20 minutes for each pound of oven-ready weight, plus a further 20 minutes. Baste every 20 to 30 minutes and uncover the breast for the final 15 minutes, to brown.

Stuffings for Roast Chicken

While it is not, of course, absolutely necessary to stuff a chicken, this has long since been a traditional way of serving poultry. The intensive breeding of birds has brought them within the range of everyone's pocket but it is undeniable that the full, rich flavour of the free-running farm bird is lacking, and stuffings have therefore taken on added importance.

You can, if preferred, simply put a sprig of rosemary in the cavity to impart a delicate flavour. But the use of different stuffings at different times will give more variety to your menu and, since the stuffings themselves are in the main not expensive to make, they have a distinct economy value in making the chicken meat go further.

See also Stuffing (page 19).

FORCEMEAT

4 ounces white bread-crumbs
1 ounce suet
2 teaspoons parsley
¼ teaspoon grated lemon rind
1 rasher streaky bacon

1 egg
pinch dried thyme
salt
pepper

Chop the parsley finely, chop or shred the suet, and chop the bacon. Mix the dry ingredients with a fork, then bind with the egg, previously well beaten. Do not pack the mixture too tightly into the bird but allow room for swelling during cooking and thus prevent the stuffing from becoming too stodgy.

HERB AND RELISH STUFFING

4 tablespoons white bread-crumbs

2 tablespoons mixed herbs (parsley, thyme, chives, marjoram)

1 small onion

2 tablespoons cranberry and orange relish

1 egg

salt

pepper

Chop the onion finely and put in a basin, together with the bread-crumbs, herbs and cranberry relish. Mix well, season to taste with salt and pepper, then bind with the egg, previously beaten, and add a little orange juice if necessary.

This stuffing is equally suitable for duck or turkey, but in the latter case you would need to increase the quantities by using either half as much again of each ingredient, or double.

CELERY AND PARSLEY STUFFING

4 ounces white bread-crumbs

1 teacup chopped celery

1 ounce butter

pinch thyme

2 teaspoons parsley

$\frac{1}{4}$ teaspoon grated lemon rind

1 rasher streaky bacon

1 egg

salt

pepper

Finely chop the parsley, chop the bacon, mix them together in a basin with the bread-crumbs, thyme and seasonings. Cook the chopped celery gently in the melted butter for about five minutes, then add all to the crumb mixture. Stir in the lemon rind, then bind the mixture with the egg, previously beaten.

LIVER STUFFING

liver from the chicken

2 ounces calves' or lambs' liver

4 ounces white bread-crumbs

1 rasher streaky bacon

1 ounce suet (chopped or shredded)

$\frac{1}{2}$ teaspoon lemon juice (optional)

1 egg

1 medium onion   salt
1 teaspoon chopped parsley   pepper
½ teaspoon dried thyme   ¼ teaspoon chopped garlic

Boil the onion until soft. Then chop it finely, add to the livers, also chopped. Mix with the crumbs, suet, and other dry ingredients. Season to taste, add the lemon juice, if used, then bind the mixture with the egg, previously well beaten.

MUSHROOM STUFFING

4 ounces bread-crumbs   2 teaspoons fresh parsley
1 ounce butter or margarine   ¼ teaspoon dried thyme
2 rashers streaky bacon   1 egg
2 ounces mushrooms   salt and pepper
½ teaspoon lemon juice

Melt the butter or margarine in a pan and in it cook the mushrooms very gently. Do not let them brown. When just cooked, drain and chop, and add to the dry ingredients in a basin. Pour the remaining melted butter into the mixture, add the lemon juice, season, and bind the mixture with the egg, previously beaten.

VEAL AND CHESTNUT STUFFING

6 ounces pie veal   1 egg
3 ounces chestnuts   salt and pepper
1 teaspoon Italian herbs

Cook, peel and skin the chestnuts and mince them together with the pie veal. Season well. Add the herbs and bind with the egg, well beaten. Bake 30 minutes if cooked separately.

PINEAPPLE AND RICE STUFFING

4 ounces rice   ½ teaspoon salt
1 cup chopped pineapple   a little black pepper
1 onion   1 teaspoon dried sweet basil

Cook the rice in two cups water for about 15 minutes. Drain and rinse with fresh water. Drain well and add the salt and pepper. Place the rice in a bowl, add the chopped pineapple, and the onion, previously peeled and finely chopped. Mix in the herbs.

RAISIN AND RICE STUFFING

2 ounces raisins, ready-
     stoned or seedless
2 ounces almonds
2 ounces ready-cooked rice
1 onion

salt and pepper
1½ tablespoons chopped parsley
2 tablespoons melted butter
1 egg

Blanch and chop the almonds, mix into the cooked rice and the raisins. Chop the onion finely, add to the mixture. Season with salt and pepper. Add the parsley, pour over the melted butter, mix well and finally bind with the well-beaten egg.

TANGERINE STUFFING

1 tangerine
4 ounces rice
½ teaspoon salt
1 onion
2 celery sticks

2 ounces mushrooms
1 tablespoon fresh chopped
     parsley
beaten egg

Cook and season the rice as for Pineapple and Rice Stuffing above. Chop the onion and mushrooms and fry lightly in a little oil, then add to the cooked rice. Mix in the chopped parsley and the celery sticks, finely chopped. Peel the tangerine, remove the pips, then cut the peel into thin julienne strips and the flesh into smallest possible pieces, and add to the rest of the mixture, combining very thoroughly. Bind with beaten egg.

PRUNE AND WALNUT STUFFING

3 ounces soft bread-crumbs
1 small onion (grated)
3 ounces prunes (stoned and
     chopped)
2 tablespoons chopped walnuts

1 dessertspoon butter
1 teaspoon dried thyme
salt and pepper
1 egg

Mix the bread-crumbs with the other ingredients, then add the butter, chopped into small pieces. Beat the egg, and with it bind the mixture into a handleable consistency, adding a little milk if necessary.

Hot Whole Chicken Dishes

CHICKEN LIMOUSIN

1 chicken, about 4 pounds weight	3 ounces butter
2 dozen chestnuts	4 ounces sausage meat
cooking oil	4 mushrooms (fairly large), minced
chicken stock	1 teaspoon parsley, minced
1 celery stalk	1 onion
½ teaspoon sugar	seasoning
pinch salt	

Cross-cut the chestnut shells on the flat side and heat them in a little oil in a heavy frying-pan until the shells begin to open. Peel the chestnuts and place them in a pan with the celery stalk, sugar, a teaspoon of butter, a pinch of salt and enough chicken stock just to cover. Simmer for about 20 minutes.

Meanwhile sauté the onion, chopped, in a tablespoon butter until soft and transparent. Then mix this with the sausage meat, the mushrooms, the parsley and a little seasoning. Stuff the chicken with this mixture, then brown the bird all over in 1½ tablespoons butter melted in a heavy casserole.

Place the casserole in the oven at 350° F (Gas 4) and cook uncovered for 20 minutes. Drain the chestnuts and reserve their stock. Place the chestnuts around the chicken, add half cup of the strained chestnut stock and continue to cook the chicken, still uncovered, for about an hour or until it is brown and tender. Add more stock during cooking time if it becomes necessary so that the dish will not dry out. You should have at the finish a condensed but adequate amount of sauce to serve with the bird.

WHOLE ROAST CHICKEN MARYLAND

A recipe for Chicken Maryland, using chicken joints, is to be found on page 37. Below, however, is a slightly varied version of that dish using whole chicken and one or two other ingredients to add variety. This is a very colourful dish to serve garnished as suggested for a family or a special meal.

1 roasting chicken (about 4 pounds)
2 ounces butter
¼ pint stock (preferably chicken)

salt and pepper
1 level teaspoon curry powder
3 bananas

Fritters

½ tin sweetcorn kernels (11½ ounce size)
1 egg
3 ounces self-raising flour

2 tablespoons milk
salt and pepper
frying oil or fat

Garnish

3 large tomatoes
salt and pepper

½ tin sweetcorn kernels
a little butter

Sprinkle the chicken with salt, pepper and the curry powder. Place in a roasting tin and dot with butter. Pour the stock around the bird. Roast at 400° F (Gas 6) for 1¼ to 1½ hours, basting the bird once after it has been cooking for about 15 minutes.

For the fritters, mix half the sweetcorn kernels with the egg, flour and milk into a batter, and season. Heat a little oil in a frying-pan and drop the batter in spoonfuls into the hot fat. Fry the underside until golden, then turn and fry on the other side. Lift out of the pan, drain on absorbent kitchen paper for a few moments before arranging them on a dish.

About 15 minutes before the chicken is ready for serving, skin the bananas, split them in half lengthways, and place them round the chicken. Halve the tomatoes, scoop out the centres, sprinkle with salt and pepper and fill with sweetcorn kernels. Dot with butter and place in the oven with the chicken, for about 10 minutes. To serve, arrange the chicken on a hot dish with the bananas and some of the stuffed tomatoes around it. Serve the rest with the fritters. Serve the gravy separately.

BRAISED CHICKEN AMBASSADOR

1 small chicken
8 ounces pork sausage meat
1 ounce butter
¼ pint white wine or dry cider

2 ounces chopped onion
2 ounces chopped mushroom stalks
1 level tablespoon plain flour
salt and pepper to taste

Stuff the crop end of the chicken with the sausage meat, then retruss the bird. Melt the fat in a frying-pan and quickly brown the chicken on all sides. Remove from the fat and place in a casserole just a little larger than the chicken. Next fry the onion until just tender, then the mushroom stalks. Add the white wine (or cider) and pour this sauce over the chicken. Cover closely and cook in a fairly hot oven 400°F (Gas 6) for 1 hour, or longer, depending on size (see p. 21).

To serve, remove the chicken from the casserole, place on a flat serving dish and keep hot. Strain the stock into a saucepan and add the flour blended with a little cold water. Bring to the boil, stirring all the time and simmer gently for 5 minutes. Season to taste. Serve separately or poured over the chicken. If liked, the dish can be garnished with buttered button onions and mushrooms.

CHICKEN BRAISED IN WINE

1 tender chicken (about 4 pounds)	4 shallots
	1 bouquet garni
2 tablespoons butter	salt and pepper, to taste
2 tablespoons olive oil	$\frac{1}{2}$ pint dry, white wine
4 ounces fat bacon, diced	$\frac{1}{4}$ pint chicken stock
4 ounces carrots	a little cognac

Heat the butter and oil in an iron cocotte or casserole just large enough to hold the chicken. Dice the bacon pieces and sauté in fat until golden. Remove the bacon; add the coarsely-chopped shallots and carrots and cook, stirring constantly, until the vegetables soften, then add the chicken and brown on all sides. Return the bacon bits to the pan, pour over cognac and flame. Add bouquet garni, salt and freshly-ground black pepper to taste, dry white wine and chicken stock. Cover the bird with a piece of buttered paper, cut to fit the casserole, with a small hole in the centre to allow steam to escape. Cover the casserole and simmer gently over a very low heat until tender (1 to $1\frac{1}{4}$ hours). Add more wine or a little chicken stock during the cooking if the sauce reduces too quickly.

PERNOD CHICKEN WITH FENNEL

Pernod is a favourite French drink with a unique flavour. The following recipe recommends 3 tablespoons of Pernod to be used in the closing stages of cooking, but if you are in doubt about this quantity it is suggested that you reduce this to $1\frac{1}{2}$ tablespoons in the first place and if you find that you would like a stronger flavour you can use the full amount on another occasion.

1 chicken (2½ to 3 pounds)   1 glass dry white wine
2 ounces butter   ½ teaspoon dried fennel
4 teaspoons olive oil   1 head celery
2 petite Suisse cheeses   6 leeks
3 tablespoons Pernod   salt and pepper

Mash the petites Suisses and add salt, pepper and fennel. Stuff the
chicken breast with this mixture. Wash and dice the leeks and celery.
Grease a large ovenware dish, place the chicken in it and roast in the
oven at 350° F (Gas 4) for 20 minutes. When browned, add the wine
and the oil. Spread out the vegetables in the dish and season. Cook in
the oven at 325° F (Gas 3) for 1 hour. Add Pernod 10 minutes before
serving. Serve the chicken surrounded by the vegetables.

POACHED SPRING CHICKEN WITH EGG SAUCE

1 small chicken   ¾ gill chicken stock
1 small onion stuck with   4 tablespoons dry white wine
    4 cloves   or cider
sprig of basil   2 egg yolks
sprig of parsley   1 ounce margarine or butter
sprig of tarragon   1 hard-boiled egg
1 blade of mace   1 teaspoon chopped parsley
salt and pepper

Garnish
1 hard-boiled egg   chopped parsley

Put the onion stuck with cloves, the herbs and mace inside the carcase
of the chicken, with a sprinkling of salt and pepper. Heat the stock and
wine in a thick stewpan. Put the bird in, cover the pan closely and
poach slowly for about 45 minutes, or until tender. Dish the bird and
remove the skin and flavourings. Thicken the liquor with egg yolks, at
the same time adding margarine or butter in small knobs. Add chopped
hard-boiled egg and parsley, and season to taste. Pour over the bird and
garnish with sieved hard-boiled egg and chopped parsley.

FRENCH POACHED CHICKEN

1 chicken, young and plump   2 dessertspoons salted butter
    (about 3 pounds trussed)

Court-bouillon
2 quarts chicken stock   2 slices lean bacon
2 carrots   pinch of thyme

2 small turnips   1 bay leaf
2 celery stalks   2 sprigs parsley
4 leeks   truffles (optional)

Make the court-bouillon by heating the chicken stock and in it placing the carrots, cut in pieces, turnips, quartered, the celery stalks, cut in pieces and the leeks cut up but with most of their green tops removed, the bacon and herbs. Simmer for 10 minutes and then put in the chicken and bring to simmering point. The original recipe calls for a number of slices of truffle inserted under the skin over the breast and leg meat of the bird and if you can do this, so much the better, of course.

Simmer, covered, for 30 minutes after the stock comes back to the boil. Then turn off the heat and let the chicken stand and continue to poach in the hot stock for 20 minutes. Remove the chicken to a hot platter, pour over it a little of the stock so that it will not dry out, and keep it warm. By now the vegetables should be tender. If they are not, continue to cook them while you make the sauce. In a small saucepan reduce $1\frac{1}{4}$ cups of the stock to $\frac{1}{2}$ cup over a high flame. Taste it for seasoning and then take off the heat and whip in the 2 dessertspoons of unsalted butter previously creamed. Serve the chicken surrounded by the vegetables and hand the sauce separately.

COQ AU VIN

Coq au Vin is a famous dish, but as with many classics, recipes do vary in certain respects. On page 38 you will find a Coq au Vin recipe using a bird cut into 6 pieces. The following recipe however allows for the chicken to be cooked whole. Another variation is that in this case the brandy is flamed and in the recipe on page 38 the brandy is added to the sauce.

2 to 3 pounds chicken   20 shallots
white pepper   8 ounces mushrooms
lemon juice   2 garlic cloves
5 ounces butter   1 dessertspoon plain flour
1 small wine-glass brandy   salt
1 bottle red wine

Season the chicken well with salt, pepper, garlic and lemon juice. Melt 3 ounces butter in a heavy-based saucepan and in it brown the chicken all over. Heat the brandy in a ladle, set it alight and pour it over the chicken. Move the saucepan about until the flame has died down, then add the wine and the chicken giblets. Cover with a tight-fitting lid and simmer gently for about 1½ hours. Meanwhile skin the shallots, chop them and brown them in an ounce of the butter. Add them immediately to the chicken together with the mushrooms.

When the cooking time is up, first remove the giblets, then lift the chicken, carve it and arrange the pieces on a hot dish. Beat the remaining butter into the flour and divide it into tiny balls. Drop these into the sauce and bring it slowly to just below boiling point. Stir until the sauce has thickened and pour it over the chicken pieces and arrange the shallots and mushrooms over the top. You can if you wish serve small crescents of fried bread around the edge of the dish.

CHICKEN NORMANDY

1 boiling fowl	¼ pint cider
3 cooking apples	1 teaspoon Calvados or brandy
4 ounces streaky bacon	salt and pepper
3 small onions	2 egg yolks
1 ounce butter	

Quarter and core the apples and place inside the prepared bird. Chop half the bacon and fry gently till the fat is extracted. Add the butter, melt, and then brown the chicken carefully in this fat. Transfer to a deep fireproof dish. Chop the onions finely, add to dish, with salt and pepper. Cover the bird with the remaining bacon strips, pour the cider round, cover closely and cook slowly (300° F Gas 2) for about 3 hours. When the chicken is cooked, drain off all the liquor into a saucepan. Beat in the egg yolks, stir over a very low heat until the mixture thickens, add the Calvados or brandy, then pour over the chicken and serve immediately.

TOP-OF-STOVE CHICKEN

Here is a whole chicken recipe which you can use even if you only have a gas-ring in your bed-sitter. It is easy and economical, and the bird does not shrink as much as in roast chicken.

2 ounces bacon fat, dripping or cooking oil	1 leek
1 chicken, 2–2½ pounds	1 stick celery
salt and pepper	1 teaspoon salt
sprinkling mixed spice	1 small cup stock (or ½ cup water, ½ cup wine)
1 large onion	2 ounces mushrooms
flour and cornflour	tomato purée
2 large carrots	

Melt the fat or oil in a large, heavy saucepan. Meanwhile rub the chicken well with flour, sprinkle with salt, pepper and spice. Rub well in, then brown the chicken, breast downwards, in the hot fat. Meantime chop the onion, carrots, leek and celery. Put the onion in to brown with the chicken. When the breast is well browned, turn the bird the right-side up, add all the vegetables, the salt, the stock or wine and water mixture. Cover with a really tight-fitting lid, turn down the heat, and leave the chicken to simmer till almost cooked (about 1½–2 hours). Blend 1 cup of the pot liquor with a little cornflour and a dessertspoon of tomato purée. Return it to the pot, stir till it thickens, add the mushrooms and cook a further 15 minutes uncovered.

Hot Dishes Using Chicken Joints

CHICKEN JOINTS

In many of the following recipes you are given the alternative of starting with a whole bird or with chicken joints.

Now that chicken is so conveniently packaged, you can buy whatever parts of the bird seem best suited to the dish you want to prepare, or to the particular tastes of your family. Some people prefer to eat chicken legs, others think the wing and breast meat is more delicate.

Sometimes it is more economical to buy a whole bird and joint it yourself. This way, of course, you get the giblets for making stock and flavouring a stuffing. But if you want to serve smaller chicken portions, you can buy somewhat larger quarter-chickens and divide each into half, as follows.

Leg quarter   Using a sharp knife and a cutting board, cut across the joint where the drumstick joins the thigh.

Wing quarter   Stand the quarter, breast uppermost, on your cutting board. Then with your sharp knife, cut downward. This ensures that you will leave some breast meat on the wing.

Drumsticks and   These, too, can be bought in separate packages, which
breasts   is both more convenient and more economical than
                   starting with a whole bird when using recipes intended
                   for these cuts. This is specially important in the case of
                   chicken breasts, and you will find the recipes which use
                   them grouped together on pages 47 to 52.

Whatever you use, whether it is a whole bird or portions, make sure
that the meat is thoroughly thawed out before you begin cooking.

FRIED CHICKEN

Nothing could be simpler and more straightforward than plain fried
chicken. Simply flour the quarters, either whole or divided into two
portions, as explained above, and place into two inches of hot fat in a
saucepan or sauté pan. When the pieces are brown, turn them and
continue cooking over a lower heat, with the pan uncovered. Whole
quarters will take 25 to 35 minutes to cook, according to size, and you
can, of course, add tomatoes, onion rings, or mushrooms during the
cooking process if you wish.

SOUTHERN FRIED CHICKEN

For this variation, flour the quarters or joints, then dip them first in
beaten egg and then in bread-crumbs. Fry briskly in two inches of hot
fat until crisp, then more gently until tender, taking care not to over-
crowd the pan. For a crisp finish, cook the chicken with the lid on for
the first ten minutes, then take off the lid and complete the cooking
over a moderate heat.

SOUTHERN FRIED CHICKEN WITH SAVOURY RICE

4 chicken portions or a 2 to	1 large onion
$2\frac{1}{2}$ pound chicken, jointed	$2\frac{1}{2}$ teacups stock or water (a
2 ounces plain flour	stock cube may be used)
2 ounces butter	1 level teaspoon salt
salt and pepper	2 rounded tablespoons grated
1 level teacup long grain rice	Parmeson cheese

Season the flour with salt and pepper and coat the chicken portions.
Melt the butter in a frying-pan and brown the chicken on the fleshy
side for about 10 to 15 minutes. Transfer to an ovenproof dish or plate
and cook a further 20 minutes at 400° F (Gas 5). While the chicken is

cooking in the oven, chop the onion and add it together with the rice to the butter remaining in the frying-pan. Cook over a moderate heat for 5 to 10 minutes or until the rice takes on a golden colour. Add extra butter if necessary. Stir in the stock and salt (if unseasoned stock or water is used), continue cooking over a very low heat until all the liquid is absorbed (about 20 to 25 minutes), stirring occasionally. At the end of the cooking stir in the cheese, heating only long enough to melt the cheese. Pile the rice on a large, flat dish, arrange the chicken pieces on top and garnish with parsley.

SPANISH CHICKEN WITH SAFFRON RICE

Spanish chicken

4 chicken portions or a 2 to 2½ pound chicken cut into joints
2 ounces butter
2 ounces streaky bacon
1 clove garlic, finely chopped
1 medium onion, finely sliced
4 ounces mushrooms, sliced

2 tomatoes, cut in small wedges
1 small red pepper, chopped
1½ ounces plain flour
¾ pint stock, or stock and milk mixed
3 tablespoons single cream
3 tablespoons sherry
seasoning to taste

Saffron rice

1 level teacup long grain rice
generous pinch of powdered saffron

1 level teaspoon salt
nut of butter
2½ cups of boiling water

Brown the chicken portions on the fleshy side in the butter in a frying-pan. Transfer the chicken to a casserole. Lightly sauté the bacon, garlic, onion and mushrooms in the fat remaining in the pan, then spread over top of chicken. Arrange tomato wedges over top of the mixture, then sprinkle on top the red pepper. Add an extra ½ ounce of butter to the pan, then stir in the flour and cook over a moderate heat for 1 to 2 minutes. Add the stock and bring to the boil, stirring constantly. Finally, stir in the cream and the sherry and seasoning to taste. Pour over the ingredients in the casserole, cover and cook approximately 1¼ hours at 350° F (Gas 3).

About half an hour ahead of serving time, stir the rice, salt and saffron into the boiling water in a saucepan. Cover and cook gently over a very low heat until all the water is absorbed (20 to 25 minutes). Stir in the butter and turn into a serving dish. Serve with the Spanish chicken.

CATALONIAN CHICKEN

1 chicken, 2½ to 3 pounds or 4 large joints, each cut in two	½ pint giblet stock
	4 tablespoons white wine
	1 dessertspoon tomato purée
1 ounce margarine	salt and pepper
1 tablespoon oil	½ pound chestnuts
12 button onions	½ pound sausages
1 ounce flour	fried croûtons to garnish

Remove the giblets from the chicken and simmer in a little water to make stock. Cut the chicken into eight joints. Heat the margarine and oil in a large pan and fry the joints and onions until golden brown all over. Remove from the pan and arrange in a casserole. Add the flour to the pan, stir in the stock, wine, purée and seasoning and bring to the boil, stirring. Pour the sauce over the chicken, cover and cook in a moderate oven, 375° F (Gas 5) for 30 minutes.

Meanwhile slit the chestnuts, cover with water, bring to the boil and simmer gently for 10 minutes; drain and peel. Fry the sausages until brown. Add the chestnuts and sausages to the casserole and cook for a further 15 minutes. Arrange the chicken and sausages in a warm serving dish, spoon the sauce over and garnish with the croûtons.

GRILLED CHICKEN, AMERICAN STYLE

1 chicken, about 2 pounds in weight (or 4 ready-cut joints)	pinch of nutmeg
	½ level teaspoon salt
	1½ level teaspoons marjoram— if available
1 tablespoon lemon juice	
2 cloves garlic	8 large mushrooms, roughly chopped
3 rounded tablespoons butter or margarine	parsley to garnish

Cut the chicken into four joints and rub them with lemon juice. Crush the garlic, place in the grill pan without the rack, add 2 tablespoons butter and heat until the butter is melted. Turn the joints in the butter and grill under medium heat for approximately 20 minutes, turning and basting frequently. Shortly before cooking is finished, melt the remaining butter in a frying-pan, add the nutmeg, salt and marjoram, then the mushrooms and cook gently for 5 minutes. Arrange the chicken on a flat dish with the juices poured over. Garnish with the mushrooms and a sprinkling of chopped parsley.

CHICKEN CHORON

4 chicken joints or 1 whole chicken, jointed

For the sauce

1 teaspoon shallot, finely chopped	3 ounces unsalted butter
2½ fluid ounces dry white wine	1 teaspoon tomato purée
2 egg yolks	salt and pepper
grated rind and juice of 1 small orange	few drops lemon juice
	2 tablespoons cream (optional)

Grill the chicken pieces, as in previous recipe but omit the garlic. When they are almost ready, commence making the sauce. This should be served immediately it is cooked, but you can if you wish stir in two tablespoons of cream to prevent it from separating if you need to keep it warm for a few moments. Put the shallots and the wine in a small saucepan and cook until the liquid is reduced to about 2 dessertspoons. Strain it into a bowl, add the egg yolks, grated rind and juice of the orange and the tomato purée. Place the bowl over a saucepan of boiling water, add the butter, a teaspoonful at a time and allow each piece to melt before adding the next. If there is any sign of the mixture "scrambling" take the bowl from the saucepan and drop in a teaspoon of cold water. Continue the cooking, adding cold water again if necessary, and when all the butter is used season with salt and pepper and then add a few drops of lemon juice. Pour over the grilled chicken and serve as quickly as possible.

CHICKEN WITH ORANGE AND ALMOND SAUCE

4 chicken quarters	1 level dessertspoon caster sugar
salt, pepper and paprika	
2 ounces margarine	1½ ounces almonds, shredded and browned
3 oranges	

Sprinkle the chicken quarters with the seasonings. Heat the margarine in a large pan and fry the chicken until golden brown all over. Cover the pan, reduce the heat and cook gently for 30 minutes or until the joints are tender. Meanwhile, squeeze the juice from two of the oranges, remove the skin and pith from the third and cut into segments. Remove the chicken quarters from the pan and arrange on a hot serving dish. Drain the excess margarine from the pan and add the orange juice, segments and sugar to the pan. Bring slowly to the boil, stirring, and allow to boil rapidly for 2 to 3 minutes. Adjust the seasoning, pour the sauce over the chicken, sprinkle with the almonds and serve.

CHICKENBERRY CASSEROLE

1 tablespoon corn oil
1 roasting chicken, about 3
    pounds, cut in quarters,
    or 4 ready-cut large
    chicken joints
½ clove garlic, finely chopped
    (optional)

4 level tablespoons jellied
    cranberry sauce
1 pint water
1 large packet tomato soup
2 tablespoons white wine
4 ounces mushrooms, peeled
    and sliced

Heat the corn oil in a deep pan and add the chicken and the garlic (if used). Brown the chicken quickly on both sides. Remove the chicken from the pan. Rub the jellied cranberries through a sieve and add to the saucepan with water and contents of the packet of tomato soup. Bring to the boil, stirring. Stir in the wine and replace the chicken. Cover and cook gently for 30 minutes. Add the mushrooms and continue cooking for a further 15 minutes. Place the chicken on a serving dish and pour the sauce over.

BAKED SUSSEX CHICKEN

4 chicken portions
salt
3 ounces butter

1 clove garlic, crushed (optional)
2 packets potato crisps
1 ounce grated Cheddar cheese

Preheat oven to 350° F (Gas 4). Sprinkle the chicken joints with salt. Melt the butter in a saucepan with the crushed garlic, if used. Crush the potato crisps with a rolling pin, then mix them with the cheese. Dip the chicken pieces in the melted butter, then coat each piece evenly with the crushed crisps and cheese mixture. Arrange the chicken in a single uncrowded layer in a shallow baking tin. Remove the garlic from any remaining butter and trickle the butter over the pieces. Bake, uncovered, on the middle shelf for approximately 40 minutes. This is delicious served hot accompanied by a crisp, green salad.

CHICKEN MARENGO

1 roasting chicken, 2 to 2½
    pounds
1 lemon
4 ounces mushrooms
1 clove garlic
½ cup brown stock

1 tablespoon tomato purée
3 tablespoons olive oil
1 large wine-glass white wine,
    Madeira or sherry
salt and cayenne pepper
parsley and thyme

Joint the bird neatly and brown the pieces in the hot olive oil for about 10 minutes. Remove, and prepare the sauce by stirring in the tomato purée, stock, garlic (chopped finely), sprig each of parsley and thyme, wine, salt and pepper. Replace the chicken, cover and cook on a low heat for 45 minutes. Next, add the mushrooms, and juice of half a lemon. Cook for a further 20 minutes. Remove herbs and serve in a deep dish garnished with fried bread croûtons, sprigs of watercress and thin halved lemon slices.

NORMANDY CHICKEN (CASSEROLED VERSION)

chicken joints
1½ ounces butter or margarine
1 fair-sized onion, or several
    small ones
2 to 3 cooking apples

2 rashers bacon
¼ pint cider
salt and pepper
thyme, parsley, bay leaf

Melt the butter in a pan, brown the chicken joints all over, then take out and lay aside. Slice the onion, fry gently for 5 minutes, then add the bacon, cut finely, and the apples, previously peeled, cored and rough-cut. Cook till the mixture turns colour, then transfer to a casserole, together with the chicken joints, alternating in layers. Season well, pour in the cider, adding a little water if necessary. Add a sprig of thyme, two sprays of parsley and half a bay leaf. Cover closely. Cook for 1 to 1½ hours at 300° F (Gas 2).

This recipe assumes the use of a whole bird, jointed. For a smaller quantity, purchase half a bird or individual joints and reduce other ingredients accordingly.

CHICKEN MARYLAND

1 young chicken
little flour
1 egg
bread-crumbs

butter, margarine or bacon
    dripping
salt and pepper

Garnishes
1 medium banana per person

Corn fritters
1 cup flour (bare)
1 cup sweet-corn (either
    frozen, or scraped from
    cobs)
1 teaspoon baking powder

1 egg
salt and pepper
½ cup milk
cooking oil or fat

Joint the bird, and roll in the flour seasoned with salt and pepper. Coat with egg and bread-crumbs, and fry gently for about 35 to 40 minutes in fat not less than $\frac{3}{4}$ inch deep. When tender and golden brown, lift and drain well. Serve with the bananas, sliced lengthways and fried in butter or margarine, and accompanied by corn fritters, made as follows.

Mix flour, salt and baking powder together. Beat the egg, add a dash of pepper and a little milk. Make a well in the flour and pour in the egg mixture, beating gradually and forming a batter. Add milk for correct batter consistency, then stir in the sweet-corn. Drop tablespoonfuls of the mixture into a little hot fat or oil. Cook till golden brown on both sides. Drain well before serving.

WEST INDIAN CHICKEN

1 young chicken (about 2 pounds)	$\frac{1}{2}$ pint boiling water
2 onions	1 teaspoon curry powder
4 ounces butter	small bunch mixed herbs
2 green peppers	(thyme, parsley, tarragon,
1 tablespoon flour	1 bay leaf)
3 tablespoons dessicated coconut	pinch of saffron
	salt, pepper, and a good pinch of cayenne

Joint the chicken, and season with the salt, pepper and cayenne. Melt half the butter in a deep pan, and in it brown the chicken pieces. In another pan, fry the onions and peppers, both sliced. When they, too, are lightly browned, sprinkle the chicken joints with flour, transfer the onions, peppers and butter, and cook gently, allowing the flour to brown, too.

Make, meanwhile, some coconut milk by pouring the half-pint of boiling water on to the dessicated coconut, allow to stand for 15 to 20 minutes, then squeeze liquid through muslin. Pour the coconut milk into the pan, add the herb bouquet, the curry powder, and the saffron already soaked in a little hot water. Mix well, cover closely, and allow to simmer gently for about 45 minutes. To serve, place pieces on a dish, pour the sauce over them, and serve with plain rice, boiled and well dried.

COQ AU VIN

1 cockerel ($2\frac{1}{2}$ to 3 pounds)	4 to 6 ounces mushrooms
4 rashers bacon	4 ounces butter
4 ounces spring onions	2 tablespoons flour

1 to 2 cloves garlic
bunch of mixed herbs
½ bottle Burgundy or other
    good red wine

½ pint (approx.) stock or water
glass of brandy
salt and pepper

Melt about 3 ounces butter in a deep pan. Dice the bacon and fry it, together with spring onions, till they are golden brown. Cut the cockerel into pieces (not more than 6), rub each with flour. Add to pan, sprinkle with a little flour, and allow to brown. Next, add the mushrooms and continue cooking for a few moments. Pour in the wine a little at a time, then add the stock or water, already heated. The cockerel pieces should now be just covered with liquid. Add the garlic (ready crushed), the bunch of herbs, and pepper and salt to taste. Cover with lid, and allow to simmer for about 30 to 45 minutes or until the bird is cooked. Meanwhile mince the cockerel's liver.

When ready, lift out the cockerel pieces and arrange in a serving dish. Remove the bunch of herbs, strain the liquid, and transfer the onions and mushrooms to the dish. Make a roux with 1 ounce butter and 1 tablespoon flour, add the stock and stir till it thickens. Boil gently to cook the flour, then remove from heat and add the minced liver. Stir well and, finally, add the brandy. Reheat, but do not let the sauce boil again. Pour the sauce over the cockerel, and serve.

Variations

While a young cockerel is preferable for this dish, an older bird or a boiling fowl may be used. In that case, extend the simmering time accordingly.

The brandy can be omitted altogether, or can be added to the pan before the wine and stock, and fired. If you have been able to reserve the blood of the bird, this should be added with the liver and brandy.

CHICKEN MORNAY

4 joints of roasting chicken
bread-crumbs
2 ounces butter
2 ounces flour
½ cup chicken stock

½ cup milk or cream
2 tablespoons grated Parmesan
    cheese
seasoning

Make a roux by melting the butter and blending in the flour. Cook gently for 5 minutes, taking care not to let the mixture turn brown. Then add the stock gradually, stirring all the time. Season to taste. Cook a further 3 minutes, then draw from flame and gradually add the milk or cream. Return to a very low heat, cook again for 2 or 3 minutes, then stir in the grated cheese. Dip the chicken joints in this sauce, then roll them in bread-crumbs until thoroughly coated. Fry the pieces in butter or margarine until tender. Serve with French fried potatoes and lettuce hearts tossed in French dressing.

HUNGARIAN PAPRIKA CHICKEN

2½ to 3 pounds chicken, or 4 chicken joints
1 medium onion
1 green pepper
4 tomatoes (ripe)
1 heaped tablespoon Hungarian paprika

1 teaspoon plain flour
¼ pint stock
3 ounces pork dripping
5 ounces sour cream (or fresh cream soured with juice of half a lemon)
salt and pepper

Melt the pork dripping in a large, heavy pan, and in it fry the onion, finely chopped, until transparent. Take the pan off the heat and stir in the paprika. If using a whole chicken, cut into four and add this together with the giblets to the pan (otherwise use your chicken joints). Add the pepper and tomatoes, quartered, with the stock and bring to the boil. Simmer for about 45 minutes or until the chicken is tender, seasoning with a teaspoon of salt. Remove the chicken pieces from the pan and keep hot. Add to the sauce a half teaspoon white pepper and the cream and flour mixed together. Cook gently for about 5 minutes, then sieve finely. Reheat the sauce and pour over the chicken pieces.

INDIAN CHICKEN CASSEROLE

A 2 pound bird or 4 chicken joints
1½ level teaspoons powdered ginger
1 level teaspoon salt
2 pounds onions
5 tablespoons butter or ghee
1 level tablespoon turmeric

1 clove garlic
1 cardamon
½ level tablespoon cumin
1 level tablespoon coriander
¼ pint yoghurt
½ pint water
5 peppercorns

Skin the chicken or chicken joints. Prick all over with a fine skewer, rub in the ginger and the salt and leave for 30 minutes. Chop half the onion and fry in the ghee or butter until evenly brown. Stir into the onion the clove of garlic, already crushed, then lift the onion from the pan and drain. Take the seeds from the cardamon and cook them in the fat briefly, then add the chicken together with the turmeric, cumin, coriander, and yoghurt and cook until the yoghurt is almost dry. Pulp the cooked onion, add the water and pour this mixture over the chicken joints. Thinly slice the remaining onions. Put them on top of the chicken mixture together with the peppercorns and transfer the whole dish to the oven, tightly covered. Cook at 325° F (Gas 3) for about one hour. An enamelled iron casserole is ideal for cooking this dish. If you have no suitable receptacle to use both on top and inside the stove, start the dish in a frying-pan and transfer to a casserole at the point where the pulped onion is to be poured over the chicken pieces.

Note Ghee is clarified butter and is used in Indian cooking in preference to any other kind of fat. To make ghee, melt butter in a pan over a low heat. When it comes to the boil, sprinkle with a little cold water, to check the froth. When the sizzling ceases, throw in a sprig of mint and a bay leaf. Heat for a few moments longer, then strain. When cool enough pour into a jar and keep, covered, in the refrigerator.

INDIAN CHICKEN PILAU

1 chicken, about 2 to 2½ pounds
6 ounces butter
2 onions
2 cloves garlic
12 ounces rice
½ pint yoghurt
1 teaspoon cinnamon
4 cloves
4 or 5 peppercorns
3 or 4 cardamoms
1 small teaspoon salt
pinch of saffron
3 eggs
water or chicken stock

Hard-boil the eggs, and reserve for garnish. Parboil the rice, drain and reserve. Joint the chicken neatly. Melt the butter in a strong saucepan. When hot, add the onions, thinly sliced, and cook till golden brown. Remove onion rings and reserve. Now put the chicken joints into the butter and brown lightly all over. Add the salt, peppercorns, cloves, cinnamon and garlic (previously crushed into a cup of water). Then add the yoghurt, together with sufficient water or chicken stock to simmer the chicken. Allow to cook gently for about 15 minutes, then add the rice, sprinkle with the cardamom seeds and cover very closely. Simmer for about 30 minutes, or until rice and chicken are cooked. Just before the rice is cooked, sprinkle it with the saffron soaked in a tablespoon of boiling water. Remove to serving dish, and garnish with onion rings and slices of hard-boiled egg.

SPANISH PAELLA

Half a chicken	1 or 2 cloves garlic
chicken bouillon cube	saffron stalks (or powder)
12 ounces long grain rice	6 to 8 black olives
3 tomatoes	olive oil
2 onions	$1\frac{1}{4}$ to $1\frac{1}{2}$ pints hot water
2 peppers (red or green)	shellfish (see below)
1 small tin peas	salt and pepper

Paella ingredients can be varied according to pocket and inclination, but ideally it should contain several varieties of shellfish—shrimps, prawns, cockles, mussels, crab or lobster meat, oysters—about 2 cupfuls in all. The olives are optional; the peas can be fresh, frozen or tinned; a small quantity of chopped bacon may also be added, and so can one or two Spanish spiced sausages (*chorizos*). Runner beans, coarsely chopped, can be substituted for peas, or a mixture of both may be used. Paella should be cooked in a large flat pan and served direct from it. If nothing suitable for table use is available, cook in a heavy frying-pan and transfer to a preheated serving dish.

Cut the chicken into 3 neat portions. Make a chicken stock with the hot water and soup cube. In a little of the liquid soak 2 saffron stalks (or a good pinch of powdered saffron) ready for use later. Pour about $\frac{1}{4}$ inch of olive oil into the bottom of the pan. Add the crushed garlic (1 or 2 cloves, according to preference) together with the onions, peeled and sliced, and sauté for a few moments. Add the chicken pieces, brown lightly on both sides, then add the olives, the tomatoes, sliced, and the peppers, sliced after removal of pith and seeds. If using runner beans or fresh peas, put them in at this stage. Then add the rice, stirring to prevent burning, till the rice changes colour. Pour in the stock gradually, allowing the rice to absorb the moisture. Add the saffron colouring, salt and pepper to taste, and simmer the mixture over a low heat, stirring from time to time. When the rice is almost cooked, add the shellfish and the tinned or frozen peas (thawing them first). Continue cooking till rice is cooked, then transfer to serving dish if necessary. Garnish with a few shrimps and peas, and bring to the table piping hot.

Note If bacon or *chorizos* are used, they should be added at the same time as the chicken.

BENGAL CURRY

4 chicken joints	2 onions
1 clove garlic	$\frac{3}{4}$ pint stock
3 ounces butter or ghee	salt

1 level tablespoon curry powder	small quantity milk
2 level tablespoons tomato purée	a few almonds
	1 small apple

Melt the butter and in it brown the chopped onions and finely chopped garlic clove. Add the apple, chopped and unpeeled. Divide the chicken quarters in half and add to the pan. Next put in the almonds, curry powder, purée, seasoning, 1 tablespoon milk, stock, and simmer gently uncovered until the chicken is tender and cooked. The liquid will reduce to a thick gravy. Serve on boiled long grain rice, together with chutney, peas and chopped hard-boiled eggs.

VIENNESE CHICKEN

1 small roasting chicken or 4 chicken joints	1 tablespoon tomato purée
2 onions	$\frac{1}{4}$ pint stock
3 rashers bacon	$\frac{1}{4}$ pint sweet vintage cider
1 ounce butter	salt and pepper
1 teaspoon paprika	2 tablespoons cornflour
	1 clove garlic

Melt the butter in a large pan, brown the chicken joints then add the onion, chopped, bacon, chopped and the garlic, crushed. Cook gently for 10 minutes, then add the tomato purée, stock, cider, salt and pepper. The chicken joints should just be covered. Place the lid on the pan and cook very slowly for 1 to 1½ hours. When ready to serve, lift the chicken pieces from the sauce and place on a serving dish. Blend the cornflour with 2 tablespoons cold water and stir into the sauce in the pan. Bring it to the boil, stirring constantly. Cook for 2 minutes after the sauce has thickened, then pour the sauce over the chicken pieces.

AMERICAN SMOTHERED CHICKEN

1 chicken or 4 joints	$\frac{3}{4}$ cup dry vermouth
1 heaped teaspoon paprika	$\frac{3}{4}$ cup cream
3 ounces butter or chicken fat	a little milk

Cut the chicken into 8 pieces and shake them in a paper bag with a mixture of pepper, salt and flour. Make sure that every piece is well coated. Brown the chicken in the butter or fat and arrange in a large casserole. Sprinkle generously with paprika, then pour over the vermouth, cream, the juices of the frying-pan, and enough milk almost to cover the chicken. Bake uncovered at 375° F (Gas 5). Turn the chicken pieces occasionally and stir the sauce which should be thick and curd-like. Cook until the chicken is very tender and almost leaving the bones, then serve on rice, either plain boiled, or fried in butter with a little onion and a pinch of herbs.

FRENCH SPRING CHICKEN PIQUANTE

half a spring chicken (*poussin*)
   per person
1 tablespoon Worcester sauce
1 tablespoon tomato purée
1 teaspoon grated onion
1 clove garlic
bay leaf

pinch of basil
3 ounces butter
4 tablespoons vinegar
3 tablespoons red wine
½ teaspoon paprika
salt and pepper

Wash, dry and brush each half bird with melted butter. Melt 2 ounces butter in a saucepan, blend into it the tomato purée, the Worcester sauce, the onion, garlic and basil. Add the bay leaf and simmer gently for two or three minutes. Then, add the vinegar, salt and pepper to taste, the paprika and, lastly, the wine. Simmer for a further 3 to 4 minutes. Place the halved birds on a greased grill rack and cook briskly until golden. Then reduce the heat and continue cooking. Baste continuously with the sauce. When the birds are quite cooked, strain the sauce, pour over and serve immediately.

GERMAN CHICKEN IN BEER

4 chicken joints
8 ounces German pork sausage
2 large onions
a little flour

salt
freshly ground black pepper
1 ounce lard
1 pint light ale

Skin and slice the onions, skin and cut the sausage into 4 pieces. Mix the salt and pepper into the flour and toss the chicken pieces in the mixture. Melt the lard in a pan, brown the chicken joints all over, transfer them to a casserole. Fry the onions in the remaining fat, adding a little extra if required. When the onions are golden brown, add to the casserole, put in the sausage pieces and pour over the casserole any remaining fat in the pan. Pour half the ale into the frying-pan, bring slowly to the boil, and stir and scrape round the pan to incorporate any small pieces which remain. Allow the beer to boil for 2 minutes, then pour over the ingredients of the casserole together with the rest of the pint of ale. Cover and cook in a slow oven 300° F (Gas 2) for about 1½ hours. Finally, raise the heat high and cook for a further 10 minutes, uncovered.

SWEET AND SOUR CHICKEN

4 chicken joints	1 tablespoon wine vinegar
1 pound new potatoes	1 tablespoon brown sugar
2 ounces flour or cornflour	1 teaspoon ground ginger
1 small can concentrated orange juice	1 large orange
	$\frac{3}{4}$ pint chicken stock

Season the flour or cornflour and shake the chicken joints in it. Fry the pieces until golden brown on either side and place in a casserole. Mix together the orange juice, vinegar, sugar, ginger and stock. Pour over the chicken, cover and cook for 30 minutes at 350° F (Gas 4). Next, add the potato and cook for a further 45 minutes. Meanwhile remove the rind and pith from the orange, cut the rind into thin strips and the flesh into slices. Place on top of the chicken and cook the dish for a final 15 minutes.

HOT CHICKEN BAKE

2 ounces margarine	2 tomatoes
1 jointed chicken	1 medium onion
8 ounces skinless pork sausages	salt and pepper
4 rashers bacon	chopped parsley

Melt the fat in a small baking tin. Lay in the jointed chicken, cut side uppermost, baste and cook in a hot oven, uncovered, for 10 minutes (425° F, Gas 7). Meanwhile cut the sausages into $\frac{1}{4}$ inch rounds, mix with the chopped bacon, the skinned and sliced tomatoes, and finely chopped onion and the seasoning. Remove the chicken from the oven, baste, and turn the pieces. Lay the savoury sausage mixture on the top and return the dish to the oven for a further 20 to 25 minutes, or until the chicken is tender. Serve garnished with chopped parsley.

CHICKEN IN ROKA DRESSING

1 uncooked chicken (or 4 joints)	1 bottle Roka Blue Cheese Dressing
2 to 3 tablespoons seasoned flour	paprika pepper

Wipe, trim and joint the chicken. Coat each piece in the seasoned flour. Dip the floured joints in the dressing until evenly covered and place in a casserole. Sprinkle the paprika lightly over the chicken, cover and place in a moderate oven 350° F (Gas 4) for 50 to 60 minutes. Remove the lid of the casserole for the last 10 to 15 minutes of cooking time to allow for browning.

CHICKEN DIANE

4 chicken joints
8 ounces pork sausage meat
1 tablespoon chopped parsley
1 small onion, finely chopped
pinch paprika
a little minced garlic or garlic salt
1 tomato, chopped
1 green pepper, finely chopped
salt and pepper
a little stock

Brown the chicken joints in butter. Meanwhile mix together in a bowl the sausage meat, parsley, onion, paprika pepper, garlic or garlic salt, tomato and green pepper. Season with salt and pepper to taste, and bind with a little stock or hot water. Grease four pieces of kitchen foil and place a portion of this mixture on each. Place a browned chicken quarter on top, sprinkle with salt, pepper and paprika and fold over to make a neat, airtight parcel of each chicken piece. Bake in a pre-heated oven at 350° F (Gas 4) for 50 minutes. Allow a little longer if the chicken quarters are particularly large. Serve with baked jacket potatoes cut open with a pat of butter inserted in each.

ANNIVERSARY CHICKEN

4 chicken quarters
4 rashers streaky bacon
4 ounces mushrooms (button mushrooms preferably)
2 small onions
2 large cups inexpensive red wine
2 teaspoons chopped parsley
salt and pepper
flour

Wash and dry the chicken pieces. Dredge with flour and brown them all over in a little butter melted in a large, heavy pan. At the same time fry the finely-chopped onion in this fat. Chop the bacon finely, add it to the pan and turn the heat down to simmering point. Add the chopped parsley, seasoning and wine and simmer uncovered until the liquid has reduced to about half. Now put in the mushrooms (whole if small, otherwise sliced), and continue cooking until the chicken is tender. This will take from 25 to 35 minutes according to the size of the joints.

TOMATO CHICKEN CASSEROLE

4 chicken portions
4 small onions
4 rashers streaky bacon
8 ounces tomatoes, skinned and sliced
1 teaspoon brown sugar
1 teaspoon vinegar
salt and pepper
oil or margarine for frying
1 dessertspoon tomato purée

Melt the fat or oil in a large, heavy pan and in it brown the washed and dried chicken portions until they are golden brown. Remove them from the pan and place them in a large casserole. In the fat frizzle the streaky bacon, cut small, then add the tomatoes, sugar, vinegar and seasonings. Simmer until the tomatoes cook to pulp, then add the tomato purée and a very little water if necessary. Pour this sauce over the chicken, cover the casserole tightly, and cook at 350° F (Gas 4) until the joints are tender (approximately 1 to 1¼ hours).

CHICKEN IN ONION SAUCE

4 chicken joints	½ pint white sauce
1 large onion	salt and pepper
a few cloves	

Fry the chicken joints in the usual way. Make your onion sauce as follows. Boil the onion, stuck with a few cloves, in water until tender. Now make half pint of white sauce with butter and flour, using a mixture of milk and onion cooking liquid. Take the cloves out of the onion, chop it coarsely and add it to the white sauce. When the chicken joints are cooked, pour over them this onion sauce and serve with green peas and baked potatoes or mashed potatoes that have been buttered and browned under the grill.

Hot Dishes Using Chicken Breasts

One of the benefits of modern marketing methods is that chicken breasts can now be bought in separate packets. These delicacies are used in the following recipes, but you can, of course, buy a whole bird or two and cut off the breasts, using the legs and remaining carcase to make other recipes in this book.

Chicken breasts are known as *Suprêmes de volailles*, and we start off with the classic French dish of this name.

CHICKEN BREASTS SUPREME

2 chickens	salt and pepper
2 egg yolks	fine bread-crumbs
6 tablespoons butter	$\frac{1}{2}$ cup cream
6 tablespoons oil	4 ounce can button mushrooms
3 tablespoons flour	nutmeg
$\frac{3}{4}$ cup chicken stock	

Remove the breasts from the bones and take off the skin. Separate the small fillets from the large ones, and pound them all flat between sheets of waxed paper. Season the fillets with salt and pepper, dip them lightly in flour, then in an egg yolk beaten with 1 teaspoon of water, then in fine bread-crumbs. Heat together the butter and oil, and brown the chicken breasts in this rather slowly, over moderate heat, for about 3 minutes each side, or until they are golden brown. Remove the chicken to a platter and keep it warm. Strain the fat in the skillet into a small bowl, wipe the skillet clean, and return to it 2 tablespoons of the clear fat. Blend in 1$\frac{1}{2}$ tablespoons of flour and add gradually the chicken stock and cream. Simmer, stirring, until the sauce thickens somewhat. Add a dash of nutmeg, and salt and pepper if necessary. Add mushrooms, drained. Mix 1 egg yolk with a spoonful of the sauce, add this to the sauce, and reheat it, stirring, without letting it boil. Pass this sauce suprême in a sauce-boat.

CHICKEN BREASTS IN PORT SAUCE

2 packets frozen chicken breasts	1 ounce butter
1 carrot	7 medium mushrooms (optional)
1 large onion	1 ounce flour
2 cloves	1 tablespoon port
sprigs of thyme or parsley	5 tablespoons cream
1 pint stock	salt and pepper
	chopped parsley

Defrost chicken breasts. Slice the carrot and onion, place in pan with cloves, chicken, herbs and seasoning. Cover with stock. Cover closely and simmer for about 45 minutes or until tender. When chicken is cooked, lift out the pieces and lay in the serving dish. Keep hot. Meanwhile melt the butter in a pan (lightly fry the mushrooms if used and remove from pan). Stir in the flour and lightly cook for a few minutes to form a roux. Strain the simmering liquid into the roux gradually, stirring all the time. Simmer 5 minutes. Add the port wine, mushrooms and stir in the cream. Heat through and check seasoning. Pour over chicken and sprinkle with chopped parsley.

CUMBERLAND CHICKEN

1 packet frozen chicken
   breasts
2 ounces butter
2 tablespoons lime juice
1 dessertspoon red-currant
   jelly

3 tablespoons lemon juice
¼ teaspoon dry mustard
pinch ground ginger
few drops tabasco sauce
1 rounded teaspoon cornflour
salt and pepper

Season the defrosted chicken with salt and pepper. Grill for 12 to 15 minutes, turning and basting frequently with the butter and lime juice. Meanwhile, combine the jelly, lemon juice, mustard, ginger and tabasco sauce. Remove the chicken to a hot serving dish, combine the sauce with the drippings in pan, and thicken with the cornflour, slaked with a little water. Bring to the boil and cook, stirring, for a few minutes. Pour sauce over chicken, serve hot. (Serves 2.)

CHICKEN BREASTS AU GRATIN

4 chicken breasts
4 slices Gruyère or Cheddar
   cheese
4 slices ham

1 egg
bread-crumbs
1 tablespoon flour
oil or fat for frying

Slit the chicken breasts in half lengthways. Make a "sandwich" filling with the ham and cheese. Season the flour and dip the filled breasts in it and then in beaten egg and bread-crumbs. Fry in hot fat or oil until crisp and golden brown, then lower the heat and cook the breasts steadily for about 15 minutes. Serve with hot vegetables or, if preferred, with a salad.

CHINESE CHOP SUEY

6 to 8 chicken breasts
1 large tin bean sprouts
4 ounces bamboo shoots
5 water chestnuts
4 ounces mushrooms
1 large or 2 small onions
3 tomatoes

2 tablespoons cooking oil (or
   cooking fat)
1 teaspoon cornflour
½ cup water
½ teaspoon salt
1 tablespoon soy sauce

Cut the bamboo shoots into thin slivers and then into narrow strips. Shred the chicken finely. Cut the mushrooms into thin slices, chop the onion finely, dice the water chestnuts and slice the tomatoes. Heat the oil in a frying-pan, fry the chicken, sprinkled with salt, for about 3 minutes. Remove from pan. Now fry the onions, mushrooms, bean sprouts and tomatoes for a few minutes, turning constantly. Add the bamboo shoots, and water chestnuts. Fry until ingredients are cooked and fat is absorbed. Mix cornflour into the water. Pour into frying-pan, together with soy sauce. Add the shredded chicken. Stir all together, cook for further 2 minutes or until thoroughly hot, then serve immediately.

CHINESE FRIED CHICKEN WITH PORK

sliced breasts from 1 large chicken	3 level tablespoons soy sauce
16 ounces pork	1 level dessertspoon cornflour
3 ounces mushrooms	4 ounces bamboo shoots
5 water chestnuts	1 tablespoon cooking sherry
3 eggs	cooking oil or fat

Cut the pork and the chicken into thin slices of roughly equal size. Cut the bamboo shoots into strips (as for Chop Suey), put in a mixing bowl together with the water chestnuts and mushrooms, both finely chopped. Add the cornflour, soy sauce, sherry and the egg whites, just lightly beaten. Stir all ingredients together thoroughly. Beat the egg yolks separately. Prepare cooking oil or fat for deep frying. Spread each slice of pork with a teaspoonful of the prepared mixture, and place a slice of chicken on top to form a "sandwich". Dip the sandwiches in the beaten egg yolks, and fry in the hot, deep fat until golden brown. Serve very hot.

CHICKEN KIEV

4 chicken breasts	1 large or 2 small eggs
6 to 8 ounces unsalted butter	flour
1 cup fine bread-crumbs, preferably brown	oil or clarified butter for deep frying

Skin the breasts if necessary and flatten them with a rolling pin until thin like escallops of veal. Cut the butter, which should be thoroughly chilled, into sticks, place one in the middle of each chicken slice, and fold it over so that the butter is entirely enclosed. Tie with cotton to secure. Sprinkle each chicken parcel with flour, then dip into beaten egg and coat with the bread-crumbs. Work quickly so that the butter inside the chicken breasts does not have a chance to soften.

Meanwhile, have ready a deep pan with smoking hot oil or clarified butter. To test whether the temperature of the frying agent is correct, drop into it a small cube of bread which should brown in just over a minute. You may, if you prefer, use a piece of raw potato, and this should quickly fry into a perfect chip. When you have the temperature right, arrange the chicken rolls in a frying basket and lower into the pan. Fry quickly for about 5 minutes until the chicken is golden brown. Drain thoroughly. Remove the cottons before serving and serve very hot.

You may, if you wish to introduce another flavour, soften the butter first, blend into it a tablespoon of chopped parsley and then rechill in a roll shape, or you may chop 2 ounces mushrooms very finely and blend those into the butter before making the parcels.

CHICKEN BREASTS IN TOMATO WINE SAUCE

3 whole chicken breasts
3 dessertspoons butter
2 dessertspoons olive oil
1 onion, finely chopped
4 dessertspoons flour

$1\frac{1}{2}$ cups chicken stock
$\frac{3}{4}$ cup thick tomato juice
salt and pepper
$\frac{1}{4}$ cup dry sherry
2 dessertspoons chopped parsley

Skin, bone and halve the breasts. Brown them slowly on both sides in the hot butter and oil. Remove from the pan and put on one side. Lightly brown the chopped onion in the same pan, blend in the flour, then pour on the stock and tomato juice. Stir until the mixture comes to the boil, then season with salt and pepper. Add the chicken, sherry and parsley and simmer, covered, until the chicken is tender, about 30 minutes. These ingredients are sufficient for about 6 servings.

CHIC HULLOA

1 (10 ounces) packet frozen
    chicken breasts, defrosted,
    skinned and boned
1 egg
bread-crumbs, seasoned with 1
    teaspoon curry powder
salt and pepper
garlic powder
1 clove garlic, crushed

$\frac{1}{2}$ ounce butter
1 cup pineapple juice
$\frac{1}{2}$ cup white wine
juice 1 large lemon
    (2 tablespoons)
1 ounce cornflour
curry powder
1 teaspoon sugar

Rub chicken with clove garlic, dip in egg and bread-crumbs and fry in butter until golden brown; remove from pan, but keep warm. Wipe grease from pan. Combine the pineapple juice, wine, lemon juice, cornflour, garlic powder, curry powder and sugar and cook slowly until sauce thickens. Place chicken in the sauce, cover and let simmer for 25 to 30 minutes. Serve with rice and vegetables to choice.

CHICKEN AMANDINE

3 ounces quick-cooking macaroni
1 packet frozen chicken breasts
    or thighs
1 carrot
1 onion
pepper and salt
1 bay leaf
1 ounce butter
2 tablespoons finely chopped
    onion

$\frac{1}{2}$ ounce plain flour
$\frac{1}{4}$ pint double cream
$\frac{1}{4}$ pint chicken stock, or water
    and bouillon cube
1 red pimento, shredded
$\frac{1}{2}$ green pepper, shredded
1 tablespoon chopped parsley
1 ounce almonds, shredded

Cook macaroni as directed, and drain. Cover the chicken with cold water. Add salt, pepper, carrot, onion and bay leaf. Simmer until cooked. Fry the chopped onion in butter; stir in flour and cook a few seconds. Add stock and cream, stir until thick and cooked, but do not allow to boil. Add the chicken pieces, macaroni and all the remaining ingredients. Pour into a greased casserole and bake in moderate oven, 375° F (Gas 5), for 15 to 20 minutes.

CHICKEN LOUISE

2 cold roasted chickens
1 tin chicken consommé
1 tin cream of chicken soup
2 envelopes gelatine

4 thick slices ham
1 tin goose liver pâté
8 tarragon leaves
2 truffles (optional)

Soften the gelatine in $\frac{1}{2}$ cup consommé and set aside. Heat the remaining consommé to boiling point, pour over the gelatine mixture. Stir until dissolved. When cool add the cream of chicken soup, well beaten and strained. Cool but do not allow to set. Meanwhile carve four breasts with wings attached from the two chickens, draw off the skins. You can use the remaining chicken for any of the other salad recipes in this section or for making mousse. Dress the breasts (which are called Suprêmes) on ham, trimmed to the same size as the Suprêmes. Spread with goose liver pâté. Place them on a grill tray wire mesh and pour a thin layer of the gelatine mixture over them. Chill, and repeat until all the Suprêmes are well coated. Keep the gelatine soft enough to spread by placing it over tepid water. Decorate the tops with the sliced truffles if used, and crossed tarragon leaves. Serve very cold.

CHICKEN ANNA

4 slices ham (thick)
4 Suprêmes of chicken (see recipe Chicken Louise)
2 envelopes gelatine

$\frac{1}{2}$ cup port wine
1 cup mayonnaise
1 cup cream of chicken soup

Soften the gelatine in the port wine and dissolve in the chicken soup which you have first brought to the boil and strained. Lay the chicken Suprêmes on the ham slices, add well beaten mayonnaise to the gelatine mixture and spread over the Suprêmes. Chill, and serve on a bed of green peas and salad.

Hot Dishes Using Left-overs

BÉCHAMEL CHICKEN ON WAFFLES

1 ounce butter
1 ounce flour
$\frac{1}{2}$ pint milk
cold cooked chicken

1 tablespoon cream
stuffed olives
waffles—fresh made or frozen
seasoning

Make a roux by blending the flour carefully into the melted butter. Add the milk very slowly, taking care to avoid lumps. Put in a good pinch of salt and when thoroughly mixed, simmer for 10 minutes. Add the cream. Next, mix in the shredded cooked chicken, using sufficient to give a good spreading consistency which is not too runny. Heat thoroughly but do not boil. Spread on to crisp, freshly-toasted waffles, and garnish with sliced, stuffed olives arranged in a row right across the top.

HOT CHICKEN MOULD

8 ounces left-over chicken
4 ounces ham
2 tablespoons flour
2 ounces butter or margarine

6 tablespoons chicken stock, or milk
1 large egg or 2 small ones
seasoning
pinch of basil

Mince the chicken and ham, add seasoning and basil. Melt the butter or margarine and blend into it 2 level tablespoons flour. Gradually add the stock, bring to the boil and simmer for 5 or 6 minutes. Draw from the heat and leave to cool for 10 minutes. Then stir in the eggs, previously well beaten, add the minced meat and mix thoroughly. Grease a mould and turn the mixture into it, pressing well down. Cover with grease-proof paper tied firmly into position, place in a steamer and steam for an hour.

For sauce

1 ounce butter or margarine
1 ounce flour
½ pint stock, or milk

salt
½ cup tomato purée or pulp

Make the sauce by melting the ounce butter or margarine in a saucepan. Blend in the flour, making sure the mixture is smooth and does not brown. Add a pinch of salt, then gradually add the stock or milk. Bring slowly to the boil, simmer for 8 to 10 minutes. Heat the tomato pulp or purée separately, and when the white sauce has cooled a little, mix together carefully to avoid curdling. Turn out the mould on to a dish and pour the sauce over.

CHICKEN AND MUSHROOM CREAM

1 ounce butter
cold cooked chicken
cup of white sauce
3 ounces mushrooms

slices of toast
watercress or parsley
seasoning

Make a white sauce with cornflour, milk and a pinch of salt. See previous recipe for method. Blend in the chicken, ready cut fairly small. Melt the butter, fry the mushrooms gently till soft. Chop, then mix in with other ingredients. Season well, and spread the mixture on slices of buttered toast, garnishing with the watercress or parsley.

CHICKEN IN MARROW

1 medium-sized vegetable marrow	2 teaspoons mustard (dry)
left-over chicken (about 8 ounces)	1 dessertspoon mango chutney
6 tablespoons milk	salt
1 tablespoon curry paste	cayenne
2 tablespoons tomato ketchup	1 egg
	1 teaspoon flour
	dripping

Cut a slice off the top of the marrow, peel it and scoop out all the seeds. Boil in salted water for 10 minutes, then lift and drain. Meanwhile, make a sauce by blending the tomato ketchup, mustard, chutney, curry paste, salt, dash of cayenne, and the milk. Mix in the left-over chicken, finely minced, and bind with the egg, previously well beaten. Pack the mixture into the marrow cavity, replace the 'lid' and put in a greased fireproof dish. Dot with dripping, sprinkle the flour from end to end, and bake in a moderate oven 350° F to 375° F (Gas 4–5) until brown and cooked. Make a gravy with some stock (chicken stock preferably) and some brown gravy thickening powder. Serve very hot.

CHICKEN POPETTES

6 ounces minced chicken	$\frac{1}{2}$ pint milk
2 ounces streaky bacon	4 ounces flour
$\frac{1}{2}$ teaspoon chopped parsley	salt and pepper
2 eggs	lard

Grill the bacon till crisp, then chop finely. Mix with minced chicken, parsley, salt and pepper, and bind together with one of the eggs, well beaten. Roll into 8 balls. Flour lightly. Make a batter with the flour (adding a pinch of salt), milk and second egg, beating very thoroughly till of a creamy consistency. Put knobs of lard into bun tins and melt in a hot oven. Place a ball of mixture in each, reheat briefly, then add batter to each. Cook until well risen and golden brown in colour.

STUFFED TOMATOES

4 large tomatoes	3 to 4 tablespoons minced cold chicken
2 rashers bacon	large knob butter
1 egg	pinch of basil
2 tablespoons fine bread-crumbs	pepper and salt

Grill the bacon till crisp. Chop finely. Melt the butter, mix in the bacon, bread-crumbs, chicken, salt and pepper. Slice the tops off the tomatoes and scoop out the flesh very carefully. Sieve or mash the flesh and add to the mixture, together with the basil. Bind with the egg, well beaten, and fill the tomatoes with the mixture. Sprinkle the tops with bread-crumbs, replace the lids, dot with butter or margarine and bake in a moderate oven for 15 to 20 minutes. Serve on crisp, fried bread.

STUFFED GIZZARDS

This recipe, and the one which follows it, are old Scottish methods of putting the more neglected parts of chicken to the best possible use. They presuppose the use of large, farm-bred chickens, rather than the small broilers for which most of the recipes in this book are eminently suitable.

chicken gizzards	dripping
forcemeat stuffing	

Slit the gizzards open sufficiently wide to allow you to clean out the insides thoroughly. Prepare a forcemeat stuffing, and pack it into the apertures. Skewer firmly together, and bake in dripping in a fairly hot oven until tender.

GRANDMA'S CHICKEN CRISPIES

neck of chicken(s)	salt

For this old-fashioned titbit you require the neck only of a large fowl. Split the neck open, and pull out the yellow fat which is to be found inside. Render the fat down to clarify it, then strain. Stretch the neck out into a flat strip. Salt it lightly, then cut into small squares. Fry the squares in the hot, clarified chicken fat until they are brown and crisp.

STUFFED PEPPERS

4 peppers (red or green)	6 to 8 mushrooms
1 cup minced or diced chicken	1 ounce butter
½ cup minced or diced ham	bread-crumbs
1 small onion	1 egg
½ teaspoon minced parsley	salt and pepper

Cut the tops off the peppers at the stem end. Remove all seeds and fibres. Place in boiling water and parboil the peppers for about 5

minutes. Lift from water, turn upside down and leave to drain. Cook
the mushrooms gently in half the butter until soft, then chop finely.
Grate the onion, and mix it well together with the minced chicken,
ham and parsley. Add the chopped mushrooms, season to taste, then
bind the mixture with the egg which has been previously well beaten.
Pack the filling carefully into the peppers, top with bread-crumbs and
dot with the remaining butter. Grease an oven dish, and pour into it
enough hot water to cover the bottom. Set the peppers in the dish and
bake in a moderate oven, 350° F (Gas 4) for about 20 minutes or
until the peppers are tender.

CHICKEN CROQUETTES

cold cooked chicken (about
    8 to 10 ounces)
1 small onion
2 to 3 mushrooms
1 heaped teaspoon chopped
    parsley

knob butter or margarine
2 egg yolks
seasoning
bread-crumbs

For sauce
1 ounce butter
1 ounce flour
2 gills milk or stock

1 teaspoon lemon juice
seasoning

Make sauce by melting the butter in a pan, mixing the flour smoothly
in and cooking for 5 to 6 minutes. Add milk or stock, bring to the boil
and simmer for 5 minutes. Remove from the heat, leave to cool slightly,
then add lemon juice and seasoning.

Mince or dice the chicken, using as much white meat as possible.
Melt the knob of butter in a pan, add the onion and mushrooms,
finely chopped. Cook gently till soft, then add chicken and the binding
sauce. Mix thoroughly, then add seasoning and parsley. When the
mixture is cool, add a well beaten egg yolk. Turn on to a plate to get
quite cold, then divide the mixture into short, fat sausage-shaped
croquettes, coat with egg and bread-crumbs and fry in deep fat.

SAVOURY CHICKEN OMELETTE

For each person
2 eggs
salt and pepper
1 tablespoon milk
½ teaspoon chopped fresh parsley

cold chicken, chopped or
    minced
butter

Beat the eggs lightly, add salt, pepper, parsley, milk and a few pieces of butter. Warm the minced chicken a little by putting on a plate and standing on a pan of hot water. Melt a large knob of butter in an omelette pan, and pour in the egg mixture when the fat is hot but not smoking. Cook till almost set, then spread the chicken over one half of the omelette. Fold over and serve immediately, garnished with watercress.

CHICKEN RISOTTO WITH BACON

6 ounces rice	1½ pints chicken stock or water
1 onion	10 to 12 ounces cooked chicken
2 ounces mushrooms	8 rashers streaky bacon
2 ounces butter or margarine	salt and pepper
2 tablespoons tomato purée	

Wash the rice and drain well. Prepare and chop the onion and mushrooms. Melt the butter in a pan and lightly fry the rice, onion and mushrooms. Add the tomato purée, then gradually pour in the stock or water. Season and bring to the boil, stirring all the time. Reduce the heat and simmer gently until the rice has absorbed all the liquid and is tender (about 35 minutes).

Meanwhile cut the chicken into small pieces. Add to the rice when cooked and heat through over a gentle heat. Remove the rind from the bacon rashers, and form them into rolls. Place on skewers and grill until crisp and lightly browned. Turn the risotto on to a warm serving dish and garnish with the bacon rolls.

SAFFRON CHICKEN RISOTTO WITH PEPPERS

1 large onion	1 large or 2 small peppers
2 ounces butter or margarine	cooked chicken carcase and
8 ounces rice	giblets
1 pint chicken stock	salt and pepper
pinch of powdered saffron	lemon juice
3 ounces grated Cheddar cheese	cooking oil
1 tablespoon grated Parmesan cheese	

Melt the butter or margarine in a shallow fireproof casserole and in it fry the onion, thinly sliced, until transparent. Then stir in the rice and fry till pale biscuit coloured. Add enough stock to float the rice, then cover and simmer gently. Stir frequently adding more stock as it becomes absorbed until the rice is just tender. Stir in enough saffron to colour the rice a delicate yellow. Cut the meat from the chicken carcase into small pieces and chop the liver, heart and gizzard. Add to the rice mixture and heat through. When thoroughly heated, take from the flame and stir in the grated cheese. Season to taste with salt and pepper and a little lemon juice. Cut the pepper in half, remove the stem and seeds, brush with oil and grill on both sides until lightly browned. Cut the pepper into wedges and arrange round the rice.

CHICKEN CURRY

6 to 8 ounces cooked chicken
2 ounces margarine
1 level tablespoon curry powder
1 medium onion, finely sliced
$\frac{1}{2}$ large cooking apple, finely chopped
2 ounces plain flour
1 level teaspoon turmeric

1 pint chicken stock
1 tablespoon mango chutney
1 tablespoon sultanas
salt and pepper
8 ounces Patna rice
4 slices lemon
1 banana, sliced
a few sultanas and raisins

Melt the margarine in a sizeable pan, add the curry powder and onion and cook slowly together until the onion is almost tender. Then add the chopped apple and cook for another 5 minutes. Stir in the flour and turmeric, then add the chicken stock, and stir the pan over a gentle heat until it comes to the boil and thickens. Simmer this sauce for a few minutes, then add the chutney and sultanas, and season with salt and pepper. Now stir in the chicken which has been fairly finely cut, and heat it through but do not let it actually come to the boil. Meanwhile, put the rice into boiling salted water, boil steadily for 12 to 15 minutes until the grains are tender. Strain, separate the grains to remove the excess starch, reheat, then arrange the rice round the edge of a warm serving dish and pour the curry into the centre. Garnish with slices of lemon and the sliced banana mixed with the remaining raisins or sultanas.

CHICKEN STUFFED PEPPERS

4 green peppers
1 ounce butter
1 medium onion

4 ounces mushrooms
6 ounces cooked chicken
1 small tin tomato soup

Cut the tops off the peppers, scrape out the seeds and the core. Blanch, by putting them into cold water and bringing them up to the boil. Pour off the boiling water, rinse the peppers in cold water and place in a fireproof dish. Melt the butter and fry the onion and mushrooms, add the chicken and sufficient tomato soup to bind the mixture together. Put the mixture into the peppers. Cover with a lid or tinfoil and cook at 375° F (Gas 5) for 30 to 40 minutes.

CHICKEN PANCAKES
Pancake batter

4 ounces flour
1 tablespoon oil or melted
    butter

1 egg yolk
½ pint milk

Filling

1 ounce butter
2 ounces mushrooms
¾ ounce flour
1 gill stock
6 to 8 ounces cooked chicken

1 hard-boiled egg
1 teaspoon chopped parsley
1 tablespoon cream
salt and pepper

To garnish

1 ounce melted butter
1 tablespoon grated cheese

chopped parsley

To prepare batter
Sieve flour, add oil and egg and milk slowly and beat hard to obtain a smooth batter. If possible, allow to stand in a cool place.

To prepare filling
Melt the butter, finely chop the mushrooms, and add to the butter with salt and pepper. Cover and cook for a few minutes. Add the flour and cook till it bubbles and then add the stock and, stirring, bring up to the boil. Add the shredded chicken meat, chopped hard-boiled egg, parsley and cream. Keep warm.

Fry about a dozen pancakes and put a spoonful of filling in each and fold over and arrange them overlapping down a buttered dish for serving. Sprinkle over with a little extra melted butter and scatter over the cheese. Brown under the grill. Sprinkle with the chopped parsley.

CHICKEN AND TOMATO PANCAKES
Pancake batter
As for the recipe above

Filling

4 to 5 ounces cold chicken	1 small onion
2 rashers streaky bacon	salt and pepper
2 tomatoes	

This recipe will make even the smallest amount of chicken do for four people. Make the filling by mincing or finely chopping the onion and frying it with the bacon, chopped, in a little fat until golden brown. Add the chicken finely minced and the tomatoes, chopped, season and simmer gently until soft and well blended. Make a batch of pancakes well beforehand and let them get quite cold between sheets of grease-proof paper. Place a spoonful or two of the chicken mixture in each pancake. Roll up. Arrange in a lightly greased ovenware dish, sprinkle with salt and bake in a moderate oven until the pancakes are heated through and their edges are crisp.

CHICKEN PASTIES

Filling

$\frac{1}{2}$ ounce margarine	4 ounces cooked potato, diced
1 large onion, chopped	1 level dessertspoon chopped
$\frac{1}{2}$ ounce flour	parsley
$\frac{1}{4}$ pint chicken stock	salt and pepper
6 ounces cooked chicken, diced	

Short crust pastry

6 ounces plain flour	$1\frac{1}{2}$ ounces lard
pinch of salt	1 to 2 tablespoons water
$1\frac{1}{2}$ ounces margarine	

Filling

Melt the margarine and cook the onion until tender, add the flour and cook for a further 2 to 3 minutes. Stir in the stock and bring to the boil, stirring continuously, then simmer for 3 to 4 minutes. Add the chicken, potato, parsley and seasoning to the sauce and mix well. Allow to become cold.

Pastry

Sift the flour and salt into a bowl and rub in the fat until well blended. Mix to a stiff dough with the water. Roll out the pastry to $\frac{1}{10}$ inch thick and cut three rounds 7 inches in diameter. Divide the filling into three and place in the centre of each round. Damp the edges, and seal across the centre, pinching the edges together. Brush with beaten egg or milk and bake in a moderately hot oven, 400° F (Gas 6), for 25 to 30 minutes. Serve either hot or cold.

CHICKEN AND SCONES

Filling

1 tablespoon corn oil
1 small onion, chopped
½ green pepper, chopped
2 ounces mushrooms, sliced
1 ounce cornflour

2 tablespoons whole berry
    cranberry sauce
¾ pint milk or stock
8 ounces cooked chicken, cut
    in cubes
seasoning

Scone topping

7 ounces plain flour
1 ounce cornflour
pinch of salt

2 level teaspoons baking powder
¼ pint milk
2 tablespoons corn oil

To make the filling

Heat the corn oil and sauté the onion, pepper and mushrooms. Stir in the cornflour and cranberry sauce and cook for 1 minute, stirring throughout. Add the milk or stock and continue cooking for a further 1 minute, stirring all the time. Add the cooked chicken and season to taste. Turn into an oven-proof dish and top with rounds of scone. Bake at 425° F (Gas 7) for 10 to 15 minutes.

To make the scone topping

Sieve the flour, cornflour, salt and baking powder together. Mix the milk and corn oil, stir into the dry ingredients. Roll out on a floured board to about ½ inch thickness. Cut into 1½ inch rounds.

CHICKEN AND PRAWN PILAFF

2 tablespoons oil
1 large onion, sliced
4 rashers streaky bacon, cut
    in strips
2 ounces mushrooms, sliced
8 ounces Patna rice, washed
1 pint chicken stock

salt and pepper
8 ounce packet frozen peas
3 tomatoes, skinned, seeded
    and cut into strips
4 ounces peeled prawns
8 ounces cooked chicken, diced

Heat the oil in a large pan and fry the onion and bacon until tender. Add the mushrooms and rice and fry for 2 to 3 minutes. Pour in the stock, season well and simmer for 12 to 15 minutes, until the rice is tender and the stock is absorbed. Add the peas to the pan and cook for 5 minutes, then mix in the tomatoes, peeled prawns and chicken. Heat gently for 5 minutes and pile into a hot serving dish. This will serve up to 6 portions.

CHICKEN AND BACON COBBLER

1½ ounces margarine
1 medium onion, finely sliced
2 ounces mushrooms, sliced
1 ounce flour
1 level tablespoon tomato purée

1 chicken bouillon cube
¾ pint boiling water
salt and pepper to taste
½ bay leaf
8 ounces cooked chicken, diced

Bacon scone topping

6 ounces self-raising flour
2 ounces margarine
½ teaspoon salt

3 rashers streaky bacon (diced
    and crisply fried)
5 tablespoons milk

Pre-heat oven to 425° F (Gas 7). Fry the onion until golden brown and soft, add the mushrooms and cook for 2 to 3 minutes, then stir in the flour and tomato purée. Dissolve the bouillon cube in the water and pour this stock into the pan, blend well and bring to the boil, stirring. Add the seasoning, bay leaf and chicken. Allow to simmer for 10 minutes.

Make the scone topping by rubbing the fat into the flour, add the bacon and the milk. Roll the dough out lightly and cut into 2½ inch rounds with a biscuit cutter. Transfer the chicken mixture to a casserole dish and place the scones on top. Glaze with beaten egg and bake for about ½ hour. Serve with Brussels sprouts.

CHICKEN CLARISSA

1 ounce margarine
1 ounce flour
¾ pint milk, or milk and chicken
    stock
salt, pepper and ground mace to
    taste
6 to 8 ounces diced cooked
    chicken

1 8-ounce packet frozen peas
    (cooked)
2 hard-boiled eggs, quartered
bacon rolls and triangles of toast
    to garnish

Melt the margarine, add the flour and cook for 2 to 3 minutes. Add the milk and bring to the boil, stirring continuously. Cook gently for 3 to 4 minutes, and add seasonings to taste. Add the chicken and peas to the sauce, simmer for 3 minutes then add the eggs and simmer for a further 2 minutes. Adjust the seasoning and serve garnished with bacon rolls and toast.

CHICKEN AND ORANGE OMELETTE

2 eggs	butter
pinch of salt	$\frac{1}{4}$ teaspoon grated orange rind
pinch of pepper	1–2 ounces cooked chicken
1 tablespoon water	orange juice

Lightly beat the eggs with a fork, add the seasoning, the water and the orange rind. Heat some butter in an omelette pan, pour in the mixture and cook until just set. Have ready the filling by chopping the chicken, heating it in a pan with a little butter, some pepper and a few drops of orange juice. Place the filling on one half of the omelette, fold over and serve.

CHINESE OMELETTE

12-ounce tin Chinese vegetables	salt and pepper
2 tablespoons soy sauce	2 eggs
1 heaped teaspoon cornflour	butter
8 ounces cooked chopped chicken	

Strain the liquid from the vegetables, heat it and add to the soy sauce mixed with the cornflour. Cook until smooth and thick, then add the vegetables and chicken. Season. Beat the eggs with 1 tablespoon cold water, melt a little butter in an omelette pan and make a thin omelette. Turn the chicken mixture into a small serving dish, and top with omelette.

CHRISTMAS LOGS

8 ounces back bacon

Stuffing

$\frac{3}{4}$ ounce margarine	4 level tablespoons fresh white
1 small onion, finely chopped	bread-crumbs
2 ounces cooked chicken, finely	salt and pepper
chopped	fingers of buttered toast
1 level teaspoon chopped parsley	

Cut each rasher in half. Make the stuffing as follows. Melt the margarine and fry the onion for 2 to 3 minutes, add the remaining ingredients and mix well together. Place a little stuffing on each piece of bacon, roll up and place on a baking sheet. Bake in a moderately hot oven, 400° F (Gas 6) for 15 to 20 minutes until the rolls are crisp and brown. Serve on fingers of buttered toast. These may also be served cold.

CHICKEN WITH PINEAPPLE, ALMONDS AND CRANBERRY SAUCE

1 small can pineapple pieces
1 tablespoon corn oil
2 ounces blanched almonds
1 onion, finely chopped
¾ ounce cornflour
1 chicken stock cube

2 tablespoons whole berry
  cranberry sauce
8 ounces cooked chicken, cut
  into strips
pimento

Drain the pineapple reserving the juice. Heat the corn oil. Add the almonds and lightly brown. Remove from the pan. Reserve some for garnish. Add the onion and fry until transparent. Add the cornflour, stock cube and cranberry sauce. Make the pineapple juice up to ¾ pint with water. Add to the pan and bring to the boil, stirring. Stir in the chicken, almonds and pineapple pieces. Heat through. Serve on a bed of rice and garnish with almonds.

CHICKEN À LA KING

1½ cups cold chicken, diced
  finely
3 tablespoons shredded green
  pepper
4 ounces mushrooms, chopped
1½ ounces butter or margarine
1 egg yolk

1 ounce flour
lemon juice
salt and cayenne pepper
½ cup white stock
6 tablespoons cream
2 to 3 tablespoons sherry
  (optional)

Melt the butter and in it cook the chopped mushrooms and shredded pepper. Add seasoning, stir in flour and cook for a few minutes. Then add the white stock, already heated, a dash of lemon juice and when this is blended, the diced chicken. Cook gently for 5 to 6 minutes, then draw from the heat and mix in slowly a beaten egg yolk and the cream. It is advisable to warm the egg yolk in some of the cream first, to prevent curdling. Return to the heat but make sure the mixture does not boil, then stir till it thickens. If sherry is used, add this with the stock. The mixture may be served from a fireproof dish, or piled into a pastry case, ready-baked blind, on toast, or as a filling for crisp rolls with the soft crumbs hollowed out.

TOMATOED CHICKEN ON SPAGHETTI

1 small onion
1 green pepper
2 tablespoons oil
8 ounces cooked chicken
2 tablespoons flour

¼ pint stock
14-ounce can tomato juice
seasoning
mixed herbs
cooked spaghetti

Peel and chop the onion. Remove the top and seeds from the pepper and chop it. Heat the oil and in it sauté the onion and pepper for a few minutes. Chop the chicken and add to the pan. Stir in the flour, stock and tomato juice, and bring to the boil, stirring constantly. Season to taste with salt and pepper, then stir in the herbs. Simmer for 8 to 10 minutes. Meanwhile cook a quantity of spaghetti, sufficient for four people. Drain and serve topped with the chicken and tomato mixture.

CHICKEN CUTLETS

1 boiling fowl	1 to 2 cupfuls white bread
flour or fine bread-crumbs	1 large egg
a little butter	salt and pepper
milk	

Skin the fowl and cut off all the white meat. Mince this finely. Mix with the white bread as much milk as it will absorb, then mix it with the chicken and mince again. Season with salt and pepper and bind with the lightly beaten egg. Shape the mixture into small cakes about 1 inch thick, coat them with flour or with egg and bread-crumbs and fry in butter. Brown the outsides quickly, then lower the heat and cook slowly right through. You can use the remainder of the fowl for any of the casserole or chicken stew dishes in this book.

CHINESE CHICKEN NOODLES

4 ounces egg noodles (fine)	$1\frac{1}{2}$ level tablespoons cornflour
4 ounces cooked chicken	2 tablespoons oil
2 ounces mushrooms	2 tablespoons water
2 ounces bean sprouts	2 tablespoons soy sauce
2 celery stalks	salt and pepper
$\frac{1}{2}$ pint chicken stock	

Place the noodles in a large pot of boiling water and cook fast for 10 minutes. Pour into a colander, rinse in cold water and leave to drain. Shred the chicken and vegetables, heat the oil in a saucepan, put into it the shredded vegetables, toss them well and cook for about a minute, then add the chicken, toss and cook for a further minute. Pour in the stock, stirring well. Cover the pan, lower the heat and simmer for 10 minutes. Mix the cornflour to a paste with the water and soy sauce, and add this to the pan mixture. Stir constantly until the sauce is smooth and thick. Add the seasoning, then stir in the noodles. Heat the mixture to a high temperature and then turn it into a deep dish. This quantity makes about 3 moderate-sized portions.

CHICKEN AND CELERY FLAN

4 ounces cooked chicken	2 ounces butter or margarine
2 ounces cheese (grated)	½ pint milk or mixture of milk
1 small tin celery, or 1 head of	and celery stock
celery ready braised	salt and pepper
1 onion	4 ounces shortcrust pastry
1 ounce flour	

Make the pastry, roll it out and line a flan ring. Bake blind (with uncooked beans or rice on greased grease-proof paper to prevent rising) at the top of the oven for about 15 minutes (425° F, Gas 7). When the pastry has set, take it from the oven, remove the paper and whatever agent you have used to prevent rising. Return to the oven, lower to 350° F (Gas 4) for a further 5 minutes. Meanwhile, skin and slice the onion, fry it in half the butter or margarine until golden brown. Drain the celery, chop it up small, and add to the onion. Melt the remaining fat in a pan, stir in the flour. Slowly add the liquid to make a white sauce. Bring the sauce to the boil, stirring constantly, then pour it on to the vegetables. Mix lightly and add the chicken, finely chopped, and half the cheese (grated). When all the ingredients are well combined, pour the mixture into the flan case, spread with the remaining cheese and brown it quickly under a very hot grill. This flan can be served hot with vegetables or cold with salad.

CHICKEN AND HAM PATTIES

6 to 7 ounces cooked chicken	1 egg
3 to 4 ounces lean bacon or	salt and pepper
cooked ham	8 ounces short or puff pastry
2 tablespoons flour	pinch of mixed herbs
6 tablespoons chicken stock	1 ounce butter
3 tablespoons milk	

If bacon is used, grill till cooked. Drain off fat. Cool. Mince chicken and ham (or bacon) and add herbs. Melt the butter in pan and make a roux with the flour, stirring well and cooking gently for 3 or 4 minutes, taking care not to let it brown. Next, stir in the chicken stock, with seasoning, boil for 4 or 5 minutes, and add the milk. Draw from the heat, cool slightly, then add the egg, ready beaten. Return to a very gentle heat and cook slowly for 3 minutes. Mix in the minced meat, and leave to get cold.

Meanwhile, make the pastry. Grease some patty tins and line with pastry rounds. Spoon some of the cold mixture into each, cover with pastry rounds, moistening the edges and pressing firmly together. Prick several times on top with a fork, brush with milk or beaten egg, and bake in a hot oven for 10 to 15 minutes until golden brown. Serve either hot or cold.

CHICKEN PUFFS

8 ounces flaky or rough puff pastry (home-made or ready-prepared)
2 tablespoons butter
1½ tablespoons flour
6 mushrooms

1 glass strong chicken stock or wine
6 ounces cold chopped chicken
dash lemon juice
2 tablespoons cream
pepper and salt

Heat butter, add the chopped mushrooms, and cook gently. Sprinkle in the flour, mix well, stir in liquid gradually and allow sauce to cook for a few minutes. Add the cold chicken. Remove from heat, add cream, lemon and seasoning. Allow to cool. Roll out pastry and cut into 4 inch squares. Put spoonfuls of the mixture in each and gather up dampened edges to close pastry. Brush with beaten egg or milk. Cook at 400° F (Gas 6) for 30 minutes.

ECONOMICAL CHICKEN VOL-AU-VENT

8 ounces flaky or puff pastry
cooked chicken left-overs

1 can condensed mushroom soup
a little egg and milk

Make flaky pastry to your favourite recipe or buy some ready-prepared. Cut it in half, roll out both pieces to the size of a 6-inch dinner plate. Place a saucer or large pastry cutter on one of the circles and cut round, removing the centre. Brush the underside of this hollow ring with milk then place it on the solid circle. Brush the top with egg or milk and bake in a preheated oven at 425° F (Gas 7) until golden (about 15 minutes). Meanwhile, heat the contents of the soup can and into it blend any scraps of left-over chicken you have available, chopped or minced finely. Season well and heat slowly, bringing the mixture to boiling point. Make sure this is ready by the time the vol-au-vent is cooked. Scrape out the soft paste from the middle of the cooked vol-au-vent to give you space for your filling. Pile in the soup and chicken mixture and serve immediately. The vol-au-vent case can be cooked in advance and so can the filling. When you want to serve the dish turn the filling into the vol-au-vent cavity, quite cold, and heat the whole thing through in a moderate oven.

QUICK CHICKEN PIE

8 ounces cooked chicken meat
1 can condensed mushroom soup
milk
4 ounces ham or cooked bacon
  (diced)

1 hard-boiled egg (sliced)
a few cooked peas (optional)
1 to 2 packets potato crisps
salt and pepper

Cut the chicken into bite-sized pieces. Pour the contents of the soup tin into a saucepan and dilute it with half a can of milk or milk and water. Bring to the boil, season with salt and pepper, stir in the chicken meat, the ham, egg and peas, if used. Turn the mixture into a pie-dish and top with crumbled potato crisps. Bake for about 15 or 20 minutes.

CHICKEN LORRAINE

4 ounces shortcrust pastry
½ chicken or 2 joints
1 breakfast-cup water or stock
1 large onion
1 small can unsweetened
  evaporated milk

4 ounces coarsely grated cheese
salt and pepper
1 egg
bread-crumbs

Wash and cut the chicken joints, place in a saucepan with the onion, sliced, and the water or stock. Cover and simmer until tender. Leave to cool in the stock. Meanwhile, roll out your ready-prepared pastry and line a flan case about 8 to 9 inches in diameter. Bake blind as for Chicken and Celery Flan, page 67.
Make the cheese sauce by bringing the evaporated milk to the boil, then turning down the heat to simmering point. Add the cheese, season with salt and pepper and simmer until the cheese melts. Use the chicken stock to thin this sauce. Take all the chicken flesh off the bones, chop roughly and add to the sauce. Beat the egg thoroughly and add to the chicken mixture. Pile into the flan case, top with bread-crumbs and bake for ten minutes in a moderate oven.
You may prepare this flan well in advance, but if you are cooking it from cold, then allow a little longer for it to heat through in the oven.

CHICKEN MUSETTE

8 ounces cooked chicken
3 ounces butter
4 level tablespoons flour
½ teaspoon salt
3 ounces cheese, grated

2 ounces bread-crumbs
small can evaporated milk
½ pint chicken stock
1 packet frozen broccoli
  (10 ounces)

Following the packet directions cook the broccoli and drain it. In an ovenproof dish place first the chicken meat, well diced, and the cooked broccoli. In a saucepan melt the butter, stir in the flour and salt. Gradually add the chicken stock and evaporated milk and bring to the boil, stirring all the time. Take off the flame, add the cheese, then pour the sauce into the dish. Sprinkle the top with bread-crumbs, dot with butter and bake in the upper part of the oven at 375° F (Gas 5) for about 15 to 20 minutes.

NUTTY CHICKEN

2 ounces shelled walnuts or almonds
4 ounces butter or margarine
1 large onion
1 small cauliflower
4 ounces mushrooms

2 level tablespoons flour
¾ pint chicken stock
8 ounces cooked chicken
salt and pepper
1 teaspoon soy sauce

Melt the fat in a pan and in it fry the walnuts, quartered, or the almonds, halved. When pale brown and crisp, lift the nuts from the fat, drain and reserve. Meanwhile break the cauliflower into sprigs, skin and slice the onion and coarse cut the mushrooms. Put the vegetables into the fat and fry gently until tender, about 15 minutes. Next add the chicken, cut into small pieces. Blend the flour with a little chicken stock, stir into the vegetables together with the remaining stock, seasoning and soy sauce. Blend all the ingredients gently but completely, bring to the boil and simmer for about 10 minutes. Just before you are ready to serve, stir in the nuts. Leave for another couple of minutes, then serve on to a hot dish bordered with plain boiled rice.

Dishes From Chicken Livers

SKEWERED CHICKEN LIVERS

1 pound whole chicken livers
3 dessertspoons soy sauce
1 dessertspoon brown sugar
1 dessertspoon sherry

1 teaspoon salt
dash of ginger powder
1 clove garlic
oil for deep frying

Parboil the chicken livers in salted water for 2 minutes. Make a marinade of the soy sauce, sherry, sugar, salt, ginger and the clove of garlic, crushed. Place the livers in this marinade and leave for at least half an hour and preferably 2 or 3 hours. When ready to cook, thread the chicken livers on to skewers and deep fry in oil until golden brown or grill under a hot flame.

SWEET-SOUR CHICKEN LIVERS

8 ounces chicken livers	3 tablespoons sugar
½ cucumber	1 teaspoon soy sauce
1 carrot	3 teaspoons cornflour
2 sticks celery	1½ tablespoons oil
½ teaspoon salt	small piece green ginger
½ cup vinegar	1 clove garlic, minced
2 tablespoons water	salt and pepper

Pour boiling water over chicken livers and leave for half an hour. Seed the cucumber and cut into thickish pieces. Slice the carrot and celery. Sprinkle with salt and leave for 10 minutes. Pour over them the vinegar, water and 2 tablespoons of sugar. Leave to marinate for half an hour. Drain, then add soy sauce, cornflour and remaining table-spoon of sugar to the liquid. Heat a little oil in a skillet, fry the ginger and the minced clove of garlic for a few seconds, then add the liver. Sprinkle with salt and pepper. Stir gently, cover and braise for about 5 minutes. Then pour in the cornflour and vinegar sauce and stir it until it thickens. Finally add the vegetables and cook for a further 5 minutes or until the liver and vegetables are tender.

RISOTTO OF CHICKEN LIVERS (1)

3 dessertspoons cooking oil	½ teaspoon salt
1 pound chicken livers	large pinch ground nutmeg
½ cup sliced mushrooms	1 teaspoon soya flour
3 onions	2 cups ready-cooked rice
3 celery stalks with leaves	2 heaped tablespoons grated
1 teaspoon basil	Parmesan cheese

Wash, clean and chop the chicken livers. Chop the onions and celery stalks and leaves. Heat the oil in a skillet. Sauté the livers, mushrooms, onions and celery. Remove from the pan and put on one side. In the remaining oil, stir in the salt, flour, seasonings and mix well. Add the liver mixture and the ready-cooked rice. Stir and blend thoroughly. Heat through and serve, topped with the Parmesan cheese. This is sufficient for about 6 servings.

RISOTTO OF CHICKEN LIVERS (2)

4 ounces butter	salt and pepper
8 ounces chicken livers	8 ounces long grained rice
2 ounces sliced mushrooms	2 pints chicken stock
1 large onion	4 tablespoons cooking sherry
2 pimentoes	Parmesan cheese

Chop the onion finely and fry gently in the melted butter until tender. Clean and chop the chicken livers. Add to the onion together with the mushrooms, pimentoes (diced) and seasoning. Stir in the rice and fry, stirring frequently, for about 15 minutes. Heat the chicken stock and add to it the cooking sherry. Pour over the rice and liver mixture. Cover tightly and leave to cook very gently until all the liquid has been absorbed. Serve sprinkled with Parmesan cheese.

CHICKEN LIVERS WITH YOGHURT

1 pound chicken livers	2 dessertspoons flour
2 dessertspoons good quality margarine	dash of pepper
$\frac{1}{2}$ teaspoon marjoram	good pinch of salt
$\frac{1}{2}$ teaspoon Worcester sauce	6 ounces sliced mushrooms
1 onion	$\frac{1}{2}$ cup yoghurt
	$\frac{1}{2}$ cup stock

Halve, clean and skin the chicken livers and cut into sizeable pieces. Melt the fat in a pan, mix into it the Worcester sauce and marjoram. Lay in the liver pieces and brown very gently. Lift liver from the pan and put on one side. In the pan sauté the onion until soft, blend in the seasonings and the flour. Add the mushrooms, pour in the stock, stir until the mixture simmers. Add the liver and cover. Leave to simmer for about 3 to 5 minutes. Take out about 2 tablespoons of the liquid and mix into the yoghurt, then pour the yoghurt into the pan, stirring gently but thoroughly. Heat through very slowly but make sure that the liquid does not boil. Serve with vegetables or on a bed of ready-cooked rice.

CHICKEN LIVERS ON SCRAMBLED EGG

8 ounces chicken livers	1 tablespoon soy sauce
3 ounces butter	3 tablespoons stock or water
2 ounces mushrooms	1 tablespoon single cream
1 small onion	6 eggs
1 tablespoon flour	salt and pepper

Melt 1 ounce of the butter and in it cook the onion, finely chopped. Cook gently until tender. Slice and trim the livers and mushrooms. Add to the onion and cook all together for 2 to 3 minutes. Stir in the flour. Add the stock, soy sauce and seasoning, cover and leave to cook slowly for 10 to 15 minutes. Next scramble the eggs in the rest of the butter. When just set, remove from the heat, stir in the cream and serve in individual portions with the chicken livers piled in the middle. Garnish with sprigs of parsley.

FESTIVE CHICKEN LIVERS

1 pound chicken livers	1 teaspoon made mustard
1 wine-glass dry vermouth	1 heaped teaspoon arrowroot
1 teaspoon Worcester sauce	$\frac{1}{2}$ teaspoon salt
2 tablespoons lemon juice	1 ounce butter
1 clove garlic	pinch black pepper

Blend the vermouth, Worcester sauce, lemon juice and garlic (finely chopped), mustard and seasoning. Trim, rinse and drain the chicken livers, pat dry, then place in a basin and pour over them the marinade mixture. Leave for at least 2 hours, but longer if possible. Melt butter in a pan and leave it to brown very slightly, then stir in the livers, but not the marinade. Cover and simmer until the livers are tender (about 10 minutes), stirring from time to time. Strain the marinade, stir in the arrowroot and add it to the mixture in the pan. Continue cooking stirring gently until the mixture thickens. Serve with colourful vegetables, like green peas and baked tomatoes, and with rice rather than potatoes.

LIVER AND VODKA PÂTÉ

6 ounces chicken livers	pepper
2 ounces butter	$\frac{1}{4}$ teaspoon parsley
1 onion (chopped finely)	$\frac{1}{4}$ teaspoon thyme
2 teaspoons vodka	1 bay leaf
1 garlic clove, crushed with salt	a little pepper

Melt half the butter in a pan and in it soften the chopped onion until just cooked but not browned. Add the chicken livers, well rinsed and trimmed, cook for 5 minutes. Add the garlic, herbs and pepper and cook a further 2 or 3 minutes. Turn into a basin, pound thoroughly. Add the remaining butter, already softened, and also the vodka. Beat all ingredients very thoroughly together. Pack into a mould and chill well before serving.

CHICKEN LIVER PÂTÉ

8 ounces chicken livers
2 ounces butter
1 gill stock or water
1 shallot or piece of onion

1 garlic clove
3 slices streaky bacon
salt and pepper

Place the chicken livers into the stock in a small saucepan, together with the shallot or onion and the garlic minced finely. Poach for 20 minutes. Drain off the stock and sieve the livers. Melt the butter and stir into the sieved livers. Meanwhile grease a small oven dish and line it with the bacon slices. Season the liver mixture and pack it into the prepared dish. Place in a tin of water into a moderate oven and bake for 30 minutes. Chill before serving in sandwiches or on toast or water biscuits.

CHICKEN LIVERS AU GRATIN

12 ounces chicken livers
4 ounces butter or good quality
    margarine
2 small onions
4 tomatoes
1 pinch thyme
1 pinch dill
1 teaspoon paprika powder

2 eggs
2 pounds potatoes
2 ounces grated cheese (Gruyère
    or Parmesan)
a little scalded milk
salt and pepper
breadcrumbs

Boil the potatoes until soft, drain, mash or sieve thoroughly into a purée. Add the eggs and 1 ounce butter and a little scalded milk. Keep warm until required. Wash the chicken livers, trim off fibres and membranes and cut into small pieces. Melt 2 ounces butter or margarine in a pan and sauté the chicken livers until they are golden brown. Add the onions, chopped finely, the tomatoes, peeled and sliced finely, the herbs, paprika powder, salt and pepper. Stir, and cook in the pan, uncovered, for 10 minutes.

Pre-heat the oven at a hot setting for 10 minutes. Sprinkle a fireproof dish (greased) with bread-crumbs. Place a layer of potato purée in the bottom. Spread the chicken liver mixture together with the gravy over the mashed potato. Finally spread the remainder of the potato purée on the top and cover with the grated cheese and the rest of the butter, melted. Place at the top of the oven, and leave to bake until golden brown.

CHICKEN LIVERS AND NOODLES

12 ounces chicken livers	3 tablespoons olive oil
8 ounces tomatoes	1 clove garlic
4 ounces peas	salt and pepper
12 ounces noodles	grated cheese

Cook the noodles until soft but not mushy. Drain and keep hot. Meanwhile clean and chop the livers and brown them in the oil. Add the garlic, finely chopped, and the tomatoes, skinned and quartered. Cover, and simmer over a low heat for 15 minutes. Finally add the peas, season with salt and pepper and pile the mixture on to the noodles. Serve with grated cheese.

Cold Chicken Dishes

CHAUDFROID OF CHICKEN CARDINAL

a 3 pound chicken, fresh or ready-cooked	a few drops tabasco, optional
1 pint packet tomato soup	1 teaspoon lemon juice
$\frac{1}{2}$ pint water	salt and pepper to taste
4 rounded tablespoons thick mayonnaise	a pinch of cayenne
	3 stuffed green olives
$\frac{1}{2}$ teaspoon Worcester sauce	lettuce for garnish

If using fresh chicken, cook it by boiling, steam-boiling or roasting; cool and skin. Remove the two leg joints below the drumstick. Make the soup according to the directions on the packet, but using only $\frac{1}{2}$ pint water. Leave to cool, then stir into the mayonnaise. Add the Worcester sauce, tabasco and lemon juice and season to taste. Place the chicken on a wire rack and coat with some of the sauce, making sure the bird is completely covered. Carefully lift on to a dish and garnish with lettuce leaves. Slice the olives thinly and use to garnish the chicken on the breast and drumsticks.

FRIED CHICKEN SALAD

1 chicken (about 2 pounds)
3 large potatoes
1 small tin peas
1 small tin carrots (or equivalent in fresh carrots)
1 small tin sweet-corn
1 lettuce
cucumber

3 or 4 tomatoes
1 beetroot
salt and pepper
mayonnaise
flour
sprigs of watercress
3 ounces cooking oil or fat

Joint the chicken. Roll the joints in flour seasoned with salt and pepper. Heat the oil or fat, and fry the joints, covered, for about 10 minutes. Uncover, and continue cooking until tender. Drain, and allow the joints to cool. Boil the potatoes till cooked but not soft. Cool. Dice them, and mix with the peas and carrots, ready drained. Mix in some mayonnaise sauce, then spread the mixture in the centre of a large, shallow dish (a meat dish is ideal). Arrange cucumber rings round the outside edge of dish, then arrange slices of tomatoes to overlap slightly, all the way round. Place a small pile of diced beetroot at each end. Arrange lettuce leaves on top of diced vegetables. Then, when chicken joints are quite cold, lay them on top of the lettuce and garnish with slices of tomato and sprigs of watercress. Serve with sweet-corn.

This looks decorative and appetizing and can, of course, be adapted for use with single joints of chicken if a whole bird is not required.

ITALIAN CHICKEN SALAD

1 cooked boiling fowl
1 red pepper
1 green pepper
3 tablespoons chopped sweet/sour gherkins
3 tablespoons sweet/sour onions
mayonnaise
1 tablespoon tomato ketchup

$\frac{1}{2}$ tablespoon Worcester sauce
lettuce leaves
3 hard-boiled eggs
small tin pineapple slices (or fresh sliced pineapple)
few radishes
stuffed olives

Skin and bone the chicken whilst still hot. Leave it to cool, then when cold cut the chicken meat into fine julienne strips. Wash and halve the peppers, remove all seeds and membranes. Cut the peppers into thin julienne strips. Mix with the chicken, add chopped gherkins and onions and the tomato ketchup and Worcester sauce. Blend all the ingredients in sufficient mayonnaise to make a smooth salad. Line a serving dish with the lettuce leaves, carefully washed and dried, pile on the chicken mixture and garnish with sliced hard-boiled eggs and pineapple slices. Dot the dish with radish roses and stuffed olives.

JOINTED CHICKEN CHAUDFROID

4 ready-cooked chicken joints
scant $\frac{1}{4}$ pint aspic jelly
1 teaspoon powdered gelatine
1 to 2 tablespoons cream

$\frac{1}{4}$ pint thick mayonnaise or thick white sauce made from chicken stock
garnish

Make the aspic jelly and while it is still warm use to dissolve the gelatine. Whisk the mayonnaise or chicken sauce thoroughly, and add it together with the cream into the aspic mixture. Taste, and reseason if necessary. Allow the sauce to cool. Put the chicken on a wire sieve and coat with the sauce. Leave to set. Cut away the surplus sauce from the bottom of each joint, and when thoroughly set, garnish with peas, tomatoes, hard-boiled egg or stuffed olives. It is better to bone leg and thigh joints of chicken before coating with the sauce. Serve with a colourful salad.

DEVILLED CHICKEN DRUMSTICKS

8 chicken drumsticks
$\frac{1}{4}$ pint salad oil
2 tablespoons Worcester sauce
2 rounded tablespoons tomato ketchup
1 level dessertspoon made mustard

1 level dessertspoon French mustard
1 level teaspoon caster sugar
1 level tablespoon curry powder
salt and pepper
pinch of paprika

Trim the drumsticks and score each with a sharp, pointed knife, cutting down to the bone in several places. Mix all the remaining ingredients together to form a marinade, whisk thoroughly, then pour over the chicken pieces, making sure that the marinade penetrates the cuts. Leave for several hours or overnight if possible. Turn and baste from time to time.

Drain the chicken, place the drumsticks in a baking tin. Brush with a little of the marinade and roast in the centre of a moderate oven 375° F (Gas 5) for about 30 minutes. Turn and brush liberally with the marinade from time to time. When the chicken is golden brown, take from the pan and leave it until cold. These devilled drumsticks can be served with a cocktail dip or with a salad. Wrap a small piece of foil round each drumstick tip for decoration.

TURKISH CHICKEN SALAD

1½ cups diced chicken

1 breakfast cup boiled rice

½ cup diced celery

1 tin button mushrooms

¼ cup chopped black olives

¾ cup green grapes

1 teaspoon salt

¼ teaspoon pepper

¼ teaspoon rosemary

2 teaspoons onion juice

4 dessertspoons vinegar

8 dessertspoons oil

Remove the pips from the grapes, unless they are the seedless variety. Mix together the diced chicken, rice, diced celery, button mushrooms, olives and grapes. Thoroughly shake together the oil, vinegar, onion juice, rosemary, pepper and salt and pour over the chicken mixture. Serve very cold on a bed of shredded lettuce.

CHICKEN AND CORN SALAD

1 small roast chicken (cold)

1 crisp lettuce

3 very large tomatoes

5 ounces cooked peas

5 ounces sweetcorn kernels

1 hard-boiled egg

sprigs parsley or watercress

Carve the chicken into 6 joints. Wash and dry the lettuce and arrange on a flat serving dish. Cut the tomatoes in half, remove some of the pulp and fill 3 with peas and 3 with corn. Mix remaining peas with corn and pile in the centre of the dish with slices of hard-boiled egg around. Arrange the chicken pieces radiating from the centre with the tomato cups and sprigs of parsley between them.

CHICKEN AND RICE TOSSED SALAD

8 ounces cooked Patna rice

6 ounces cold chicken

1 small onion, chopped

1 10 ounce tin garden peas

stick of celery, chopped

2 ounces rindless mature
    Cheddar cheese, cubed

2 tablespoons French dressing

a few sliced walnuts (optional)

Mix together the rice, poultry, onion, peas, celery and cheese. Toss lightly in the dressing, chill and serve, sprinkled with sliced walnuts.

DANISH CHICKEN SALAD

8 ounces cooked chicken

3 hard-boiled eggs

1 level tablespoon horse-
    radish (freshly grated)

½ tablespoon vinegar

3 tablespoons whipped cream

salt and pepper

1 large tomato

Cut the chicken into small pieces. Shell the eggs and chop them finely or mash with a fork. Mix in the vinegar and horse-radish and then blend in the cream. Add the chicken, season with salt and pepper. Mix well. Pile on to a serving dish, decorated with sprigs of parsley and thin slices of tomato.

CALIFORNIAN CHICKEN BASKETS

8 tinned peach halves
8 ounces diced cooked chicken
8 ounces boiled new potatoes,
    diced
4 ounces chopped celery
3 tablespoons mayonnaise
1 tablespoon lemon juice
1 tablespoon minced onion

good pinch pepper
$\frac{1}{2}$ teaspoon salt
few toasted almonds
1 large lettuce
few radish roses
few spring onions
parsley

Drain peach halves thoroughly. Mix the chicken, potatoes and celery in a large bowl. Stir the lemon juice, minced onion, salt and pepper into the mayonnaise, and pour over the chicken salad, turning lightly until evenly coated. Fill the centre of each peach half with the mixture. Make a bed of lettuce in a shallow dish, arrange the filled peaches on this and pile rest of chicken salad in centre. Cover with an inverted peach half. Sprinkle tops of peach baskets with toasted almonds, decorate salad with radish roses, spring onions and parsley sprigs.

CHICKEN APPLE SALAD

1 pound chicken meat, cooked
    and diced
1 head celery, sliced
4 ounces olives, black or
    stuffed
2 ounces blanched almonds
5 dessert apples, red-skinned

4 tablespoons lemon juice
1 teaspoon salt
$\frac{1}{8}$ pint double cream
3 tablespoons salad cream
1 lettuce
endive (optional)

Dice four of the apples, unskinned, and toss in half the lemon juice. Mix together the diced chicken, apple, celery, olives and the almonds, cut in slivers. Whip the cream, mix it with the salad cream and salt and mix it lightly into the chicken mixture. Chill. When ready to use, make a bed of lettuce and endive, if used, on a serving platter, and pile the mixture on top. To garnish, core the remaining apple and cut it into rings. Dip in the remaining lemon juice to retain colour, and arrange round the dish. A stuffed olive placed in the centre of the rings will add a colourful touch.

CHICKEN FRUIT AND RICE SALAD

1 apple
lemon juice
½ pound cold cooked chicken
4 tablespoons dry cooked rice
1 celery heart, chopped

1 hard-boiled egg, chopped
1 to 2 ounces stoned raisins
    or dates
mayonnaise
salt and pepper

Dice the apple without peeling it and marinade it in the lemon juice. Cut up the chicken into small pieces and mix with the rice, celery and apple. Add the egg and the raisins or chopped dates, mix with the mayonnaise, add a little seasoning and serve in a large bowl or in individual portions on crisp lettuce leaves, with other salad vegetables if desired.

RIVIERA SALAD

4 ounces Patna rice
8 ounces cooked chicken,
    diced
4 ounces black grapes, halved
    and the pips removed

2 ounces skinned and shredded
    almonds
3 tablespoons cooking oil
1 tablespoon vinegar
salt and pepper to taste

Cook the rice in fast-boiling salted water until tender, drain and rinse in cold water and allow to cool. Add the chicken, grapes and almonds. Blend the oil and vinegar together and pour this over the rice. Mix well and season to taste. Serve chilled on a bed of lettuce.

CHANTILLY CHICKEN SALAD

2 tablespoons oil
4 tablespoons white wine
juice of ½ lemon
1 pint chicken stock
4 ounces mushrooms,
    quartered
2 large tomatoes, skinned and
    quartered
bay leaf
salt and pepper to taste
1 rounded tablespoon butter

6 ounces rice
1 red pepper, cut in strips and
    blanched
1 green pepper, cut in strips
    and blanched
¼ pint double cream
½ pint mayonnaise
6 to 8 ounces diced cooked
    chicken
1 lettuce
1 hard-boiled egg

Heat the oil, wine, lemon juice and ¼ pint stock in a pan and add the mushrooms, onions, tomatoes, bay leaf and seasoning. Cover and cook gently for 6 to 7 minutes. Melt the butter in a large pan, toss the rice in this and then add the mushroom mixture and remaining ¾ pint of stock. Add the peppers, season well, bring to simmering point, cover with grease-proof paper and a lid and cook gently for 35 to 40 minutes until the liquid is absorbed. Remove from the heat and allow to cool. Fold the cream into the mayonnaise, add the chicken and adjust the seasoning. Pile the cold rice mixture in the centre of a dish and arrange the chicken on top. Lay the lettuce around and garnish with the sieved egg yolk and chopped white.

CHICKEN AND CELERY SALAD

breast of chicken	mayonnaise dressing
1 celery head	2 eggs
1 large lettuce	4 stuffed olives
salt	

Boil the eggs hard, and leave for garnishing. Arrange the lettuce leaves, washed and very well drained, in a salad bowl. Carve the chicken breast into very thin slices, lay on the lettuce, and add the inner part of the celery, washed, dried, trimmed of greenery and cut into small pieces. Sprinkle salt lightly over, then cover with a good mayonnaise dressing, preferably a home-made one. Chill in the refrigerator for 15 minutes, then garnish with sliced hard-boiled eggs and sliced stuffed olives, arranged decoratively.

CHICKEN AND PINEAPPLE SALAD

1 tin pineapple slices	1 packet frozen peas
4 to 6 ounces cold chicken	1 celery heart
1 lettuce	few chives
8 ounces lean ham	mayonnaise

Wash and well drain the lettuce. Cover a large platter or dish with it. Drain the pineapple. Allow 1 slice for each person and arrange the slices on the lettuce. Chop the remaining pineapple, dice the celery, shred the chicken meat very finely, and mix all together. Blend with some mayonnaise, and pile on to the pineapple rings. Top with a little more mayonnaise and garnish with a few chives, which have been finely chopped. Cut the ham into 3 inch strips, roll up, and arrange the ham rolls regularly around the dish. Thaw the frozen peas. They can be used uncooked or cooked and cooled, as preferred. Take care not to overcook, however, and drain them really well. Arrange in a ring round the outer edge of the platter.

As an alternative, the ham and chicken can be used uncut, and arranged in slices on the lettuce bed, interspersed with pineapple slices. The celery can be cut in strips and arranged decoratively, or served separately together with the mayonnaise dressing.

LEMON CHICKEN SALAD

6 to 8 ounces cold roast chicken	1 dessertspoon lemon juice
1 lettuce	2 tablespoons olive oil
1 egg	3 teaspoons vinegar
1 beetroot	1 bay leaf
2 tomatoes	mayonnaise
1 lemon	salt and pepper

Cut up the cold chicken finely, and leave to marinade for at least 2 hours in the olive oil, lemon juice, vinegar, pepper and salt, all mixed together first. Top with slices of lemon and the bay leaf. Stir from time to time. When ready to serve, wash and drain the lettuce, shred fairly finely, and line a salad bowl with a layer. Then add a layer of the chicken meat (first removing the bay leaf), cover with a further layer of shredded lettuce and finish with a top layer of the remainder of the chicken. Spread the beetroot, diced, and the tomatoes, thinly sliced, over the mixture, and garnish with the egg, hard-boiled and sliced. Dot with mayonnaise, or spread mayonnaise on the top layer of chicken before adding beetroot and tomatoes.

FRUITED CHICKEN SALAD

8 ounces cooked chicken, cubed	2 oranges, peeled and chopped
4 sticks celery, chopped	3 tablespoons lemon juice
2 peaches, pears or bananas, chopped	

For the sauce

1 packet savoury white sauce mix	3 tablespoons cranberry with orange relish
$\frac{1}{2}$ pint milk	$\frac{1}{2}$ pint mayonnaise
1 level dessertspoon curry powder	$\frac{1}{4}$ pint double cream lightly whipped

Mix together the chicken, celery and fruit. Sprinkle with lemon juice and chill for 30 minutes. Make up the white sauce as directed on the packet. Allow to cool. Add the curry powder, cranberry and orange relish, mayonnaise and cream. Fold the chicken in the sauce. Serve with mixed green salad.

COLD CHICKEN SOUFFLÉ

2 cups finely minced chicken
1 envelope gelatine
$\frac{1}{4}$ cup water (or chicken consommé)
1 tin cream of chicken soup

1 dessertspoon curry powder (or a little less if preferred)
1 cup whipped cream
salt and pepper

Soften gelatine with water or consommé and stir in the curry powder. Bring the chicken soup to the boil, pour over the gelatine mixture and stir until smooth and quite dissolved. Add the chicken and set on one side to cool. When cool, fold in the whipped cream, season with salt and pepper and pour the mixture into a soufflé dish. Serve with a colourful salad.

ROASTED CHICKEN SALAD

8 ounces cooked chicken meat
8 ounces diced celery
8 ounces sliced peaches
1 dessertspoon chopped onion
salt and pepper

juice of $\frac{1}{2}$ lemon
lettuce leaves
$\frac{1}{2}$ cup cooked rice
a few slivered almonds

Cut the chicken into cubes and mix with the diced celery and sliced peaches. Stir in the chopped onion, season with salt and pepper and sprinkle with lemon juice. Arrange well-washed and dried lettuce leaves on a flat serving dish. Mix the cold rice with some of the sour cream dressing (see below) and place a little on each leaf. Toss the chicken mixture in the rest of the sour cream dressing and arrange the mixture on top of the lettuce salad. Sprinkle with slivered almonds.

Sour cream dressing
$\frac{1}{4}$ pint sour cream
3 dessertspoons lemon juice
pinch of salt
pinch paprika

$\frac{1}{4}$ teaspoon dry mustard
1 dessertspoon onion, finely chopped

To make sour cream dressing
Whip the cream, add all the other ingredients and mix thoroughly.

JAMAICAN CHICKEN SALAD

½ pint mayonnaise
3 ounces seedless raisins
2 dessertspoons rum
2 ounces salted peanuts
4 ounces shredded coconut
6 dessertspoons chopped mango chutney

12 to 16 ounces diced cooked chicken
2 bananas
salt and pepper
1 large avocado pear
lemon juice
lettuce leaves

Sprinkle raisins with the rum and leave to marinate for about 30 minutes. Mix together the mayonnaise, raisins, peanuts, chutney, coconut, chicken meat and one of the bananas, sliced. Season with salt and pepper and pile on to the lettuce leaves. Peel the avocado pear, remove the stone, cut into slices, dipping them in the lemon juice to prevent discolouration. Slice the remaining banana, dip in lemon juice, then arrange the banana and pear slices alternately round the dish.

CHICKEN WITH AVOCADO

4 avocado pears
6 ounces chicken breast
½ red pepper
salt

lemon juice
mayonnaise
stuffed olives

Slice each pear in half and remove the middle core. Dice or mince the chicken, blend with a little mayonnaise, add salt to taste, and a squeeze of lemon. Chop the red pepper finely and mix into the chicken or, if preferred, shred finely and lay in criss-cross fashion after piling the mixture into the hollow of the pear. In either case, garnish with a slice of stuffed olive. Serve as an hors d'oeuvre to 8 people or with green salad as a main course to 4.

CHICKEN LOAF

3 level teaspoons gelatine
¾ pint hot water
2 chicken cubes
½ teaspoon salt
2 teaspoons lemon juice

8 ounces diced cooked chicken
4 ounces diced pineapple
3 ounces seedless grapes
4 ounces diced celery

Soften the gelatine in ¼ pint hot water. Bring the remaining ½ pint to the boil, and in it dissolve the 2 chicken cubes. Add the salt, lemon juice and then the softened gelatine. Stir until dissolved and chill until the mixture appears thickish. Then fold in the chicken, pineapple, grapes and celery and pour into a mould. Chill until firm. Turn out and serve with salad. This dish is low in calorie content and is ideal for a slimming diet.

CHICKEN GALANTINE

1 boiling chicken, 2 pounds	3 ounces bread-crumbs
4 ounces bacon	little chopped parsley
8 ounces sausage meat (or more or less as required)	1 or 2 spring onions, chopped
	good pinch mixed herbs
2 eggs	salt, pepper, cayenne

Remove all the flesh from the bird, and mince it, together with the bacon. Combine with the sausage meat, adding sufficient to make 1½ pounds in all. Beat the eggs, and add to the meat mixture. Blend well, then add bread-crumbs, onion, herbs and seasoning. When all thoroughly mixed together, form into a roll. Tie firmly into a cloth and put into a saucepan of boiling water. Boil for 2½ hours. Remove, and press firmly between two plates. Leave to cool, then take cloth off carefully. Garnish with thin strips of red and green pepper, arranged in a lattice pattern, or with thin cucumber slices topped with sliced, stuffed olives.

CHICKEN MOULD

cooked chicken	cooked peas or stuffed olives
¾ pint aspic jelly	French dressing
2 hard-boiled eggs	lettuce
2 small tomatoes	

Make the aspic jelly by following the instructions on the packet, and pour some of it into the bottom of a ring mould. Place either the cooked peas or the sliced, stuffed olives neatly in the jelly. Slice the hard-boiled eggs evenly, and slice the tomatoes thinly. Dip each slice in the aspic jelly and press to side of mould, alternating egg slice with tomato slice all the way round. Leave to set.

When firm, mix the cold chicken, already shredded, with the remains of the egg, peas and tomatoes, and fill the mould. Pour in the remaining liquid aspic. When set, turn out on to a dish, and pile into the centre the lettuce which has previously been washed, shaken thoroughly and, just before required, tossed over and over in French dressing. (See Chicken Flan for method of making this dressing, page 89.)

SUMMER MOULD

$\frac{1}{2}$ pint hot water
1 chicken stock cube
1 level tablespoon gelatine
$\frac{1}{4}$ tablespoon tabasco sauce
3 tablespoons lemon juice
5 tablespoons mayonnaise
$\frac{1}{4}$ small onion, finely chopped
2 or 3 sticks celery, chopped

1 red-skinned apple, chopped
2 tablespoons peas, cooked
2 tablespoons whole berry
    cranberry sauce
8 to 12 ounces cooked chicken,
    diced
watercress and slices red-skinned
    apple for garnish

Add the hot water to the chicken stock cube and stir well. Dissolve the gelatine in the hot stock. Stir in tabasco sauce and lemon juice. Leave to cool but not to set. When cool, gradually stir in the mayonnaise. When setting point is reached, add the onion, celery, apple, peas, cranberry sauce and chicken. Turn into a $6\frac{1}{2}$ inch ring mould and leave to set, preferably overnight. Turn out on to a serving dish and garnish with watercress and slices of apple, dipped in lemon juice to prevent discoloration.

CHICKEN AND HAM MOUSSE

12 ounces cooked chicken
4 ounces lean cooked ham
1 ounce gelatine
$1\frac{1}{2}$ gills chicken stock
1 gill cream

$1\frac{1}{2}$ gills milk
1 ounce butter
1 ounce flour
nut of creamed butter
salt, pepper, cayenne

Make a thick white sauce with the butter, flour and milk. Melt the butter, draw from flame, stir in flour. When smooth, cook gently for a few moments, then slowly add milk and cook till smooth. Leave to cool. Dissolve the gelatine in the chicken stock. Mince the chicken and the ham, and pound into it the nut of butter, ready creamed. Season with salt and pepper, add a dash of cayenne. Blend in the white sauce, then add the dissolved gelatine, taking care not to curdle the mixture. Whip the cream lightly, then fold it into the other ingredients. Turn into a mould to set. When ready for use, turn carefully on to a dish and garnish with thinly sliced cucumber and tomatoes.

CHICKEN MOUSSE

$1\frac{1}{2}$ teaspoons gelatine
$\frac{1}{4}$ cup hot water
$2\frac{1}{2}$ cups minced chicken
1 tablespoon chopped parsley
2 tablespoons chopped peppers

$\frac{3}{4}$ cup cream
1 teaspoon salt
cayenne pepper
stuffed olives

Dissolve the gelatine in hot water. Mix together the chicken, salt, pinch of cayenne, parsley and peppers and add dissolved gelatine. Whip the cream and fold into the mixture. Put in a wet mould. Chill thoroughly. Unmould on lettuce and garnish with sliced stuffed olives.

CHICKEN IN ASPIC

2 packets frozen chicken breasts, defrosted, skinned and boned
salt, pepper
pinch marjoram
½ pint aspic jelly
1 hard-boiled egg, sliced
watercress for garnish

Season the chicken pieces with salt, pepper and sprinkle with marjoram. Wrap in tinfoil, cook for approx. 20 minutes (400–425° F, Gas 6–7). Meanwhile, pour ¼ inch aspic in a tin of 8 inches diameter. When set, arrange hard-boiled egg slices on top. Add further ¼ inch jelly. Arrange the cooled chicken pieces in tin, pour in remaining jelly, and when set turn on to a serving dish and garnish with watercress. Serve with mixed salad and new potatoes.

HARLEQUIN MOULD

8 ounces cooked, diced chicken meat
1 dessert apple (with red skin)
1 level dessertspoon grated onion
1 green pepper
4 tablespoons mayonnaise
3 tablespoons lemon juice
dash tabasco sauce
3 to 4 sticks celery
stuffed olives
1 tablespoon gelatine
½ pint chicken stock
salad greens

Heat the chicken stock gently, sprinkle in the gelatine and stir, without boiling, until it is dissolved. Rinse a mould, shake well, then place slices of olive in the bottom and pour on a little of the stock, but not enough to make the slices of olive float. Chill in the refrigerator to set firm. Leave the remainder of the stock to cool, then stir in the sauce and lemon juice, whip in the mayonnaise a little at a time.

Meanwhile, chop the celery and the cored but unpeeled apple. Take out the seeds from the pepper and dice the flesh. When the stock mixture reaches setting point, carefully fold in the chopped items, the grated onion and the chicken meat. Turn into the prepared mould, leave to set until required, then unmould on to a bed of salad greens.

CREAM MOUSSE

8 ounces cooked chicken meat (minced)
¼ pint mayonnaise
¼ pint double cream
1 teaspoon celery salt

white pepper
½ pint chicken stock
2 tablespoons lemon juice
1 tablespoon gelatine
salad items to choice

Dissolve the gelatine in the stock, taking care not to boil. When cooled, stir in the chicken meat, lemon juice, flavourings and finally the mayonnaise. Whip the cream, and fold it into the mixture directly setting point has been reached. Pour into a rinsed mould and leave to set. Serve with a colourful salad of lettuce, tomatoes, beet, green peppers, etc.

SPRING CHICKEN SALAD MOULDS

1 envelope or 3 teaspoons gelatine
¼ cup hot water
½ pint salad dressing
2 cups chicken cut into small pieces
1 cup finely chopped celery

2 hard-boiled eggs
½ cup shredded almond and Brazil nuts
2 tablespoons salad oil
2 tablespoons lemon juice
salt and pepper
½ cup tinned, diced pineapple

Chop whites of eggs. Mix with chicken, celery, pineapple and nuts. Mix oil and lemon juice (or vinegar), salt and pepper; lightly add to the chicken mixture. Leave for 30 minutes. Drain off any liquid. Dissolve gelatine in hot water. Add to salad dressing and carefully stir in the salad mixture. Place in small moulds and chill. Unmould on salads. Sieve the egg yolks over the top and add a sprinkling of chopped parsley.

SUMMER CURRY

1 chicken (2 to 2½ pounds), ready cooked
10 ounces Patna rice
½ pint mayonnaise
1 head celery
1 cauliflower (small)
4 medium tomatoes
1 tablespoon grated onion

1 to 2 tablespoons curry powder (according to taste)
salt
black pepper
2 tablespoons cream
lettuce
watercress

Boil the rice in salted water until it is just soft (about 15 to 20 minutes). Drain, rinse and spread in a shallow tin or ovenproof dish. Cover with grease-proof paper and place in a low oven to dry out. Cool. Meanwhile, stir salt and pepper to taste into the mayonnaise and add the curry powder and cream. Chop the celery, separate the flowerets from the cauliflower, wash and drain, and mix these together, adding the grated onion and the chicken meat, taken from the ready cooked bird and cut into small pieces. Blend the chicken mixture with the cooked rice, then fold in the curry mayonnaise. Serve, well cooled, on a bed of lettuce and garnish with sliced tomatoes and watercress sprigs.

PICNIC PASTIES

8 ounces flour	Cooked green peas and carrots
4 ounces lard	1 tablespoon mayonnaise
cooked chicken (at least 4 ounces)	1 tablespoon chopped celery
cooked ham	salt and pepper

Make shortcrust pastry with the flour and lard. Knead well, and roll out to $\frac{1}{8}$ inch thickness. Cut into large rounds. Mince or dice the chicken and the ham, add the celery and other vegetables, varying their quantity according to how much meat you have available. Make enough mixture to spread fairly thickly across half of each pastry round. Blend the mixture with the mayonnaise, season well with salt and pepper. Place on the pastry rounds, fold over and crimp the edges firmly. Prick lightly, brush with milk or a little beaten egg if available. Place on a greased baking tray and bake in a hot oven for 10 minutes or until pastry is a golden brown. Cool on a wire tray. Serve at home with a mixed salad or on picnics with raw whole tomatoes and cos lettuce leaves.

CHICKEN FLAN

1 short pastry flan case, baked blind	2 tomatoes
2 ounces rice	minced chicken, about 2 ounces, or more if available
2 ounces cooked peas	French dressing
2 ounces cooked, diced carrots	mayonnaise
1 hard-boiled egg	garnish

Boil the rice in salted water till tender. Rinse under cold tap, drain and dry it, then mix with the cooked peas and carrots. Make some

French dressing by mixing 2 teaspoons olive oil with a good pinch of mustard and a dash of pepper and salt, then beat in a teaspoon of vinegar. Toss the rice and vegetables in the dressing and spread across the bottom of the flan. Next, spread the minced or diced chicken over the rice mixture, and coat very sparingly with mayonnaise. Top with sliced tomatoes and hard-boiled egg, also sliced. Garnish with halved stuffed olives or halved radishes and sprigs of watercress. Serve with lettuce and cucumber.

Turkey

If you prefer your Christmas turkey from your poulterer in "fresh" form (that is, not frozen), look for smooth, black legs with short spurs, bright eyes, a broad and plump breast and white flesh. Avoid birds with sunken eyes, pale or light red and rough legs, and long spurs. The best buy of all is a hen of 7 to 9 months old, hens being generally more tender than cocks and lighter boned. You will need to buy a larger "undressed" bird than a "dressed" one; allow about 3 extra pounds for the dressing. To prepare for the table, see Chicken (page 18) and proceed in the same way.

Turkey is available in frozen form all year round, and it makes its appearance at table for all kinds of special occasions. For a party meal it is good value, and by use of different stuffings or variations in cooking, can make a most welcome change. Full instructions for handling and cooking turkeys are given in the following section.

The frozen turkey halves, now becoming very popular, can be foil-roasted with any of the stuffings given in the appropriate section (though made up in half quantities, unless you enjoy eating stuffing for its own sake, as many do) or can be plain-roasted and used for many of the recipes which call for turkey meat.

These suggestions for cooking oven-ready turkeys are designed to help you enjoy the bird at its best and make cooking as trouble free as possible.

THAW COMPLETELY BEFORE COOKING (see page 17)
It is important that the bird is quite soft before you commence cooking, and the best results will be obtained when thawing takes place slowly. This will probably be governed by how much time you have between getting the bird home and beginning to cook it.

The following table gives a guide to how to deal with an average bird of 7 to 12 pounds weight. The time for smaller or larger birds should be adjusted accordingly.

Time available	*Thawing method*
3 to 5 days	Leave the turkey in its insulated box in as cool a place as possible, or remove it from the box and transfer it, without removing the plastic bag, to a refrigerator. 2 days before cooking, take it out and test it: if it is still hard, proceed as below. If it is already softening, return it to the box or refrigerator for another day.
2 days	Put the bird on a plate in a cool pantry. Keep the plastic bag on to prevent any drying out.
24 hours	Leave the bird, in its bag, on a plate in the kitchen or other fairly warm place.

12 hours or   In an emergency you can thaw the turkey quickly by
   less   keeping it immersed in warm water.

Once thawed, the meat is, of course, perishable and should not be
kept unduly long.

THE GIBLETS

Shortly before cooking, take off the plastic wrapper and remove the
neck from the body cavity and giblets from the neck cavity of the
turkey. Reserve for making stock.

STUFFING AND TRUSSING

Many stuffings are suitable for turkey. (See recipes on pages 96 to
99.) Sprinkle the cavities with salt but do not insert the stuffing until
shortly before cooking. Allow a small teacupful of stuffing for each
pound of bird. After preparing, fill the stuffing loosely into the neck end
of the bird and hold it in place by skewering the neck skin back. If
preferred, a different stuffing can be used in the body cavity or an ounce
of butter can be inserted instead. As an alternative, you can place
either a bunch of parsley and a peeled onion, or one or two peeled
apples in the cavity instead of stuffing. In this case, cook the stuffing of
your choice in a separate greased dish.

Tie the legs securely to the tail with string—no further trussing is
required.

ROASTING THE TURKEY

Preheat the oven to the required temperature (see below). Rub the
bird generously all over with softened butter. Place, on a rack if possible,
in a greased baking tin and cover with a sheet of aluminium foil or
double grease-proof paper. Three-quarters of an hour before cooking is
completed, remove the wrapping, baste the bird thoroughly and leave
to brown all over. (With a large bird it may be sufficient to cut the foil
and uncover the breast.)

COOKING TIME

Calculate the cooking time beforehand from the labelled weight which
will be found on the box or the plastic bag, using the table below. Slow
or moderate cooking is recommended, and remember that ovens vary
considerably, so be prepared if necessary to give an extra $\frac{1}{2}$ to 1 hour.
If the extra time is not needed, the bird can be kept covered in a warm
oven until you are ready to serve it.

Test to see if the turkey is cooked by piercing the thigh with a fine
skewer—the juices should be almost colourless.

	Unstuffed turkey	Stuffed turkey	
Labelled weight (pounds)	Time at 325° F (Gas Mark 2–3)	Start at 400° F (Gas Mark 6)	Reduce to 350° F (Gas Mark 4)
5 to 6	2½ to 3 hours	20 minutes	2½ to 3 hours
6 to 8	3 to 3½ hours	20 minutes	3 to 3¾ hours
8 to 10	3½ to 4 hours	20 minutes	4 to 4½ hours
10 to 12	4 to 4½ hours	20 minutes	4½ to 5 hours
12 to 16	20 minutes per pound +20 minutes	20 minutes	20 minutes per pound +45 minutes
17 to 20	20 minutes per pound +20 minutes	20 minutes	20 minutes per pound +1 hour

WHAT TO SERVE WITH TURKEY

Traditional garnishes and accompaniments include bread sauce, stuffing, chipolata sausages, roast potatoes, Brussels sprouts and giblet gravy.

BREAD SAUCE

½ pint milk
1 onion stuck with 5 or 6 cloves
1 blade mace
2 ounces white bread-crumbs
1 ounce butter

Allow onion, cloves and mace to stand in warmed milk for ½ hour. Strain, return to pan and add butter and bread-crumbs, beating well. Stir until sauce comes to boil.

LIVER AND BACON ROLLS

Cut the turkey liver into small bite-size pieces and roll each in a piece of thin streaky bacon. Impale on a skewer and cook with the turkey for the last 30 minutes.

GIBLET GRAVY

turkey giblets (except liver)
1 onion, sliced
1 carrot, sliced
1 teaspoon salt
4 peppercorns
1 stick celery
1 small bay leaf
cold water

Rinse the giblets in cold water, then place in a saucepan with the vegetables, seasoning and bay leaf. Cover with cold water, bring to the boil and simmer for 2 hours (or pressure-cook for 30 minutes). Strain, and set aside till required.

When the turkey has been transferred to a serving-dish, spoon off as much fat from the pan as possible. Pour some of the giblet broth into the pan, stirring well and scraping all the goodness from the pan. If you prefer a thickened gravy, blend a little cornflour with some cold broth, stir into the pan, simmer, stirring, for 2 minutes, before transferring to a heated sauce-boat.

Stuffings for Roast Turkey

(see also individual recipes)

FARMHOUSE STUFFING (FOR NECK CAVITY)

¼ pound streaky bacon, chopped
3 ounces butter or fat (bacon)
1 medium-sized onion, finely chopped
6 ounces stale white bread-crumbs (3 teacups)
finely grated rind of lemon

1 heaped tablespoon chopped fresh parsley
1½ level teaspoons dried thyme
salt, pepper and grated nutmeg to taste
a little milk

Melt the fat in a saucepan and fry the onion and bacon over gentle heat for several minutes. Add the bread-crumbs and stir, cooking for another minute or two. Stir in all the remaining ingredients and mix to a moist consistency with a little milk if required.

SAVOURY SAUSAGE STUFFING

1½ pounds sausage meat
1 dessertspoon mixed herbs

2 onions (finely chopped)
1 beaten egg

Mix together all the ingredients and fill into the neck cavity of the bird. Any stuffing left over can be made into sausage meat balls and baked separately.

LEMON, THYME AND MUSHROOM STUFFING

8 ounces bread-crumbs	pinch nutmeg
6 ounces suet	4 ounces chopped mushrooms
2 teaspoons thyme	4 ounces streaky bacon
grated rind and juice of 1 lemon	2 beaten eggs
salt and pepper	

Fry the diced bacon and mushrooms in a little butter, mix all the ingredients together and bind with the beaten egg. If necessary, add a little stock to make it more moist. Fill into the body cavity of the bird.

CHESTNUT AND SAUSAGE STUFFING

1 pound chestnuts, cooked and mashed	3 sticks chopped celery
	2 eggs
1 pound sausage meat	$\frac{1}{2}$ glass cream or a little milk, and
2 or 3 minced shallots—or 1 onion, cooked in butter	stock
	seasoning

Slit the chestnuts, boil in water till soft, then peel and mash. Add all other ingredients and bind together. Fill into the neck cavity of the bird.

BRAZIL NUT AND MUSHROOM STUFFING

4 ounces butter	1 medium onion
8 ounces mushrooms	$\frac{1}{2}$ teaspoon salt
2 or 3 sticks celery	8 ounces prepared stuffing mix
$\frac{1}{2}$ cup chopped Brazil-nuts	2 dessertspoons chopped parsley

Chop the mushrooms finely, dice the celery and peel and chop the onion. Melt the butter in a pan and in it cook the mushrooms, celery, nuts and onion, sprinkled with salt, for about 10 minutes. Stir occasionally. Now add the contents of the stuffing packet and the chopped parsley. Mix thoroughly. Add water or stock if necessary to make a manageable stuffing. This is sufficient for a small turkey of about 7 pounds. If you have a larger bird, increase the ingredients proportionately.

HAM AND OLIVE STUFFING

2 cups boiled rice
2 cups toasted bread cubes
2 eggs
½ cup diced cooked ham or
  bacon
½ cup chopped stuffed green
  olives
½ teaspoon salt

½ teaspoon powdered sage
½ teaspoon powdered marjoram
a little freshly-ground black
  pepper
⅛ teaspoon garlic powder
¼ cup chopped fresh parsley
½ cup chopped onion
½ cup diced celery

Lightly beat the eggs and into them add the ingredients, mixing thoroughly and adding a very little stock or water or milk, if necessary, to make a manageable stuffing. This amount is suitable for a bird up to 7 to 8 pounds. If you have a large turkey of, say, 12 to 15 pounds, double the ingredients throughout.

SWEET POTATO AND SAUSAGE STUFFING

8 ounces sausage meat
3 dessertspoons chopped onion
1 cup chopped celery
2 cups dry bread-crumbs

2 tablespoons chopped parsley
salt and pepper
sweet potatoes

Prepare and cook enough sweet potatoes to make, when well mashed, 4 cups. Put a little cooking oil in a pan and in it sauté until light brown the sausage meat, broken up gently with a fork. Lift the sausage meat from the pan, reserve, and into the pan place the chopped onion and celery, and sauté for 3 or 4 minutes. Now return the sausage meat to the pan, mix with the cooked vegetables, add the sweet potato, the bread-crumbs, parsley, and however much seasoning (salt and pepper) you require. Mix all ingredients thoroughly together. This quantity is sufficient for a turkey of about 10 pounds in weight.

PINEAPPLE AND HAM STUFFING

1½ cups minced, cooked ham
1 cup crushed pineapple
1 cup sultanas

4 cups soft white bread-crumbs
1 cup walnuts
½ cup (scant) honey

Pour boiling water on the sultanas and leave to plump for about 30 minutes. Then mix together with the ham, bread-crumbs, pineapple, walnuts (previously chopped). Slightly warm the honey and use it to bind together the other ingredients.

OYSTER STUFFING

2 ounces butter	1 egg
2 dessertspoons chopped onion	1 cup drained oysters, chopped
1 dessertspoon chopped parsley	salt and pepper
2 cups white bread-crumbs	mixed herbs

Sauté the chopped onion in the butter until pale brown, then mix in the parsley, crumbs, seasonings, oysters, and herbs. Beat the egg and use as much of it as required to bind the ingredients together. Use this stuffing for the crop of your turkey.

Roast Turkey Dishes

TURKEY BOURGUIGNON

1 turkey (about 9 pounds)	$\frac{1}{2}$ teaspoon mixed spice
8 ounces button mushrooms	bouquet garni
6 to 8 very small onions	salt
$\frac{1}{2}$ bottle red wine	black pepper
8 ounces streaky bacon	butter

Sprinkle the inside of the prepared bird with the herbs and seasoning, but do not stuff. Cover the breast with bacon rashers, overlapping them, and place the bird in a large baking dish. Chop the turkey liver and heart and place it in a saucepan with the chopped mushroom stalks, the peeled onions, whole, and the wine. Bring to the boil, simmer gently for 15 minutes, by which time the onions should be soft. Lift the onions from the liquid and reserve. Pour the hot liquid over the turkey and cook slowly as for unstuffed turkey (see page 95), basting frequently with the liquid in the pan. Within 40 minutes from the end of cooking time, remove the bacon from the breast, place the mushrooms and onions in the baking dish and continue to baste frequently. When the turkey is ready, remove to a warmed serving dish, strain the liquid and place the onions and mushrooms around the turkey. Keep warm while you put the liquid back again in the original saucepan. Add small pieces of butter, beating thoroughly until this mixture thickens slightly, then pour it into a warm sauce-boat and serve.

FRUITED ROAST TURKEY

1 turkey
2 pounds cooking apples
12 ounces dried bread-crumbs
2 ounces seedless raisins
4 ounces prunes, cooked and
    chopped
2 ounces brown sugar
1 tablespoon grated lemon rind
juice of $\frac{1}{2}$ lemon

$\frac{1}{4}$ teaspoon cinnamon
$\frac{1}{4}$ teaspoon powdered ginger
salt
freshly-ground black pepper (if
    possible)
4 tablespoons bacon dripping
4 ounces lard
1 to 2 wine-glasses cider (vintage
    preferably)

Peel, core and slice the apples, mix them with the bread-crumbs and other ingredients. Moisten with sufficient cider to make a handleable stuffing, and put it in the turkey cavity. Sew the openings. Melt the lard in a roasting tin, place the turkey in position and roast in the usual way.

TURKEY, ITALIENNE

large turkey, 12 to 16 pounds
olive oil for basting

Stuffing

turkey liver
4 ounces ham
4 ounces salami sausage
1 medium onion
6 ounces chestnut purée
8 ounces minced veal
olive oil
2 ounces white bread-crumbs

4 ounces chopped, stoned,
    cooked prunes
1 tablespoon white wine (or
    water)
pinch nutmeg
1 egg
2 ounces Parmesan cheese,
    grated

Chop the onion finely, with the ham, turkey liver, and salami sausage. Add the minced veal and chestnut purée and cook all these ingredients slowly in 1 tablespoon olive oil for a few minutes. Remove from heat and stir in the bread-crumbs, prunes, Parmesan cheese, pinch nutmeg and the egg. Add white wine or water to moisten as required, and salt and pepper to taste. (If a sweet stuffing is liked, add 1 tablespoon honey.) Wipe out the turkey with a damp cloth, stuff. Put in a baking tin and pour over a few spoonfuls of olive oil. Soak a piece of muslin in olive oil and lay over the breast of the turkey, and roast in the usual manner. Serve with a plain brown gravy from the giblets, as the stuffing is so rich, and reserve juices in a pan for a soup.

Hot Turkey Dishes

TURKEY VOL-AU-VENT

1 large packet frozen puff pastry, milk
    just thawed

Filling

1½ ounces butter
4 rashers lean bacon, cut in
    strips
4 ounces mushrooms, quartered

1 ounce flour
¼ pint stock
8 ounces cooked turkey, diced
salt and pepper

Pre-heat the oven to 450° F or Gas Mark 8. Trim the pastry into an oval shape, and with a sharp-pointed knife mark another oval ¼ inch in from the edge, cutting halfway through the pastry. Transfer the pastry to a baking sheet and lightly brush with milk. Bake for 15 to 20 minutes, or until golden brown. Meanwhile melt the butter and gently fry the bacon and mushrooms for 5 minutes, add the flour to the pan and stir in the stock and milk. Bring the sauce to the boil and simmer for 10 minutes. Stir in the diced turkey. Season to taste. Remove the lid from the vol-au-vent and scoop out any raw pastry. Fill the centre with the sauce and replace the lid. Garnish with a spring of parsley, and serve at once.

BOXING NIGHT PILAFF

2 ounces butter or margarine
1 large onion, finely chopped
8 ounces Patna rice
1 pint stock or water
salt and pepper
4 ounces cold cooked turkey,
    diced

2 ounces seedless raisins
1 pound pork sausages
a little fat for frying
1 ounce fried, shredded almonds,
    or a little chopped parsley

Melt 1 ounce butter or margarine and fry the onion gently until cooked but not browned. Add the rice, stir and fry for several minutes, add the stock and seasoning, bring to the boil then cover and cook gently for about 20 minutes. By this time the rice should be just cooked and all the liquid absorbed. Add the turkey, the raisins and the remaining ounce of butter, stir well and keep hot. While the pilaff is cooking, fry the sausages gently in a little fat for 20 minutes. Pile the pilaff in the centre of a hot dish, arrange the cooked sausages around it and garnish with the almonds or chopped parsley.

STUFFED PEPPERS

4 peppers	8 ounces cooked turkey, chopped or minced
2 rashers streaky bacon	
knob of butter	pepper and salt
small onion	pinch marjoram
4 small tomatoes	little stock
4 tablespoons bread-crumbs	

Cut a slice from the stalk end of the peppers and scoop out seeds. Parboil in salted water for 5 minutes. Make stuffing by dicing the bacon and cooking with knob of butter. Add the onion, chopped, and the tomatoes, skinned and chopped. Stir in the bread-crumbs and add the chopped or minced turkey. Add marjoram and seasoning. Moisten with stock and fill the peppers. Place a knob of butter on top and cook in a baking tin containing a little water at 375° F (Gas 5) for 20 to 30 minutes.

TURKEY BURGERS IN BLANKETS

1 pound potatoes (cooked and mashed)	2 tablespoons tomato sauce
	good pinch mixed herbs
6 ounces minced or very finely chopped turkey	1 egg
	salt and pepper to taste
1 medium size onion	butter
1 ounce rolled oats	

Melt a little butter in a saucepan and in it cook the onion, finely chopped, until soft but not brown. Put all the ingredients except the potatoes in a bowl and mix thoroughly together. Divide the mixture into four, shape into small "loaves" and place on lightly greased baking sheet. Cover each loaf with a layer of mashed potato. Mark with fork. Brush with milk or beaten egg. Bake in middle shelf moderate oven, 350° F (Gas 4) for 25 to 30 minutes.

TURKEY AND CHIPOLATA FLAN

4 pork chipolata sausages	8 ounces cooked turkey, cubed
4 rashers streaky bacon	seasonings
1 ounce margarine	tomato wedges
1 ounce flour	shortcrust pastry using 4 ounces
½ pint turkey stock and milk, mixed	flour

Roll out the pastry and line a square 7 inch shallow tin. Prick and bake blind in a hot oven (400° F, Gas 6) for 20 minutes. Meanwhile twist each sausage in half to make two small sausages and cut. Cut the rashers of bacon in half and roll up. Place on a tin with the sausages, and bake for 10 minutes. Melt the margarine in a small saucepan, stir in the flour and cook over a gentle heat for 2 to 3 minutes. Stir in the stock and milk, bring to the boil, stirring all the time, and simmer 2 to 3 minutes. Stir in the turkey, season to taste and reheat. Pour in to the hot pastry case, arrange the sausages radiating from two opposite corners, and the bacon rolls in a line diagonally from the other two corners. Garnish the dish with tomato wedges, and serve hot or cold with green salad.

TURKEY LASAGNE

¾ pound green spinach noodles	1 teaspoon sugar
½ pound cooked ham in large cubes	4 ounce tin tomato purée
½ pound cooked turkey, diced	2 ounces butter
1 red and 1 green sweet pepper	1 chicken cube
2 cooking apples, cored and sliced	salt and pepper
	good pinch rosemary
	1 heaped teaspoon cornflour

Cook the noodles in plenty of boiled salted water for 10 to 15 minutes or until just tender. Drain. Toss in a little melted butter, turn into a warm serving dish and pile up round the sides to form a nest. Cover and keep warm in the oven. Make a sauce with the tomato purée and the chicken cube dissolved in ½ pint boiling water. Add the rosemary, sugar, and seasoning to taste. Thicken with the cornflour, first mixed with a little cold water. De-seed and slice the peppers, sauté gently in the remaining butter with the apples. When tender, stir in ham and turkey. Pour the sauce over and heat through. Turn the mixture into the centre of the noodle ring. Return to oven to reheat thoroughly.

TURKEY FRICASSÉE

8 ounces left-over turkey meat	1 ounce flour
2 ounces smoked tongue	2 teaspoons lemon juice
2 ounces mushrooms	salt and pepper
½ pint chicken broth	a little chopped parsley
1 ounce margarine	

Skin and chop the mushrooms, sauté them in the melted margarine for a few minutes, then stir in the flour. Mix well, then gradually pour in the broth, and stir until boiling. Now add the lemon juice, the turkey and tongue, cut into small dice, and the chopped parsley. Season to taste with salt and pepper. Cover the pan and simmer gently for 10 to 12 minutes. Turn the fricassée into a hot serving dish. Garnish with toast fingers or triangles.

TURKEY PIE

1 pound turkey meat	1 tin condensed mushroom soup
2 rashers streaky bacon	1 packet ready-made puff
1 large onion	pastry (or home-made
2 ounces mushrooms	pastry if preferred)

Chop the turkey meat, finely chop the onion and slice the mushrooms. Mix these together with the bacon cut in small pieces, stir in the contents of the soup tin, blend thoroughly and turn into a pie dish. Cover with the pastry, thinly rolled, and brush with egg or milk. Bake in a pre-heated oven at 425° F (Gas 7) for 30 to 35 minutes until golden brown.

DEVILLED TURKEY LEGS

the legs of a cooked turkey	¼ teaspoon cayenne pepper
2 ounces melted butter	¼ teaspoon black pepper
1 teaspoon each English and	½ teaspoon salt
French mustard	a few browned bread-crumbs
½ teaspoon curry powder	

Separate the thighs from the drumsticks of the legs at the joints, making four portions. Remove the skin. Make 2 or 3 gashes in the flesh. Brush over with melted butter. Mix the mustards, curry powder, peppers and salt to a paste. Spread this paste over the turkey legs, pushing it well into the cuts. Sprinkle with browned bread-crumbs. Place under grill and cook 4 to 5 minutes each side. Add a little more butter on top of joints if necessary to prevent burning.

TURKEY MUSHROOM SAVOURY

8 ounces Patna rice	1 gill milk
4 ounces mushrooms	1 heaped teaspoon cornflour
1 large onion, chopped	2 ounces butter
12 ounces cooked turkey	sprigs parsley (for garnish)
1 chicken stock cube	¼ pint boiling water

Cook the rice in plenty of salted water, rinse, drain, and keep hot. Reserve half the mushrooms for decoration and cook whole in a little butter. Cook the onion gently in the rest of the butter until limp and transparent. Add the chopped mushrooms, cook for another minute, then stir in the cooked turkey. Dissolve the chicken cube in ¼ pint water (boiling), and moisten the cornflour with the milk. Stir together, and pour into the pan. Continue stirring and cooking gently until the mixture is smooth and thick. Pour on to serving dish, garnish with whole mushrooms and parsley sprigs.

TURKEY FRITTERS

8 ounces cooked turkey	2 to 3 tablespoons thick white sauce
2 ounces cooked ham	a little cayenne pepper, salt and breadcrumbs
1 tablespoon chopped mushrooms	thin slices of fat bacon
1 tablespoon chopped parsley	

Frying batter

2 ounces flour	1 beaten white of egg
pinch of salt	fat for deep frying
1 to 2 yolks of eggs	parsley
2 tablespoons of milk	½ pint tomato sauce
1 tablespoon salad oil	

Mince the turkey and ham, add the chopped mushrooms, parsley, and mix all into the sauce and season. Set the mixture aside until firm. Divide evenly into 6 or 8 portions, roll these into sausage shapes, using bread-crumbs to prevent stickiness, and wrap each in a very thin slice of bacon.

Batter

Mix the flour and salt together and stir in the yolk of egg and milk. Beat until smooth and add the oil. Whisk the white stiffly and fold it into the batter. Dip the fritters into the batter and fry in deep fat. Drain well and dish on to a hot platter. Garnish with parsley and serve tomato sauce separately.

SAFFRON SAVOURY

1 pound cooked turkey cut into large dice
1 tin condensed cream of chicken soup
1 large onion, chopped
2 ounces butter
2 ounces flour
1 teaspoon salt
1 tablespoon chopped parsley

½ teaspoon white pepper
good pinch thyme
½ teaspoon paprika
powdered saffron to taste
2 apples, peeled and chopped
1 green pepper, sliced in strips
6 ounces long grain rice
1 pint water

Add rice to boiling water, coloured with about half a teaspoon of saffron, or more if a strong colour is desired. Cook until tender, strain and rinse with more hot water, then spread on a serving dish. Mix the flour with the salt, pepper, paprika and thyme. Coat the turkey in the seasoned flour, and fry gently in the butter until all the pieces are evenly browned. Remove and keep hot. Add the apples, onion and green pepper to the pan and cook for a few minutes. Remove strips of pepper and keep for garnish. Add parsley and soup to pan, cook until blended into a thick smooth sauce. Spoon sauce into centre of rice, arrange turkey pieces and garnish of green pepper on top.

TURKEY AND ASPARAGUS IN CREAM SAUCE

1 tin (10½ ounces) asparagus spears
about 1 pint stock
1½ ounces butter
1½ ounces flour
¼ pint single cream or evaporated milk

1 dessertspoon lemon juice
salt and pepper
2 hard-boiled eggs, sliced
1 pound cooked turkey meat, roughly chopped

Drain the liquor from tin of asparagus and make up to 1¼ pints with chicken stock (if no stock available, use water plus chicken cube). In a medium size pan, melt the butter, stir in flour and cook gently for 1 minute. Add measured stock, stir briskly until boiling, then stir in the cream and finally the lemon juice. Season to taste and allow the sauce to simmer gently for several minutes. Reserve a few heads of asparagus for garnishing and chop remainder. Stir chicken, asparagus and 1 sliced egg into the sauce, and turn into a heated shallow serving dish. Arrange a rosette of egg slices in the centre with heads of asparagus radiating from it.

TURKEY IN WHITE WINE SAUCE

left-over turkey meat
   (preferably breast)
slices of crisp toast
2 ounces butter

4 ounces mushrooms
Parmesan cheese
chopped parsley

For the sauce

1½ ounces butter
1½ ounces flour
¼ pint single cream or
   evaporated milk

1 pint stock (made from turkey
   giblets if possible)
lemon juice
pinch rosemary
1 glass dry white wine

Place the toast slices in a flat baking dish and on them lay the turkey meat, cut into neat, thin slices. In half the butter, brown the mushrooms, and then place them on top of the turkey meat. Make the cream sauce as in the preceding recipe, but before adding the lemon juice stir in a pinch of rosemary and the dry white wine. Pour the cream sauce over the contents of the baking dish, coat with Parmesan cheese, dot with the remaining butter, and put into a hot oven to heat through and brown slightly on top.

TURKEY CHOP SUEY

8 ounces white turkey meat
3 tablespoons cooking oil
1 onion
1 to 2 cloves garlic
1 small slice ginger, or pinch
   ginger powder

½ cup celery
½ cup bean sprouts
1 tablespoon cornflour
2 tablespoons water

Sauce

2 tablespoons soy sauce
1 tablespoon sherry
½ teaspoon sugar

½ teaspoon salt
pinch pepper

Blend the sauce ingredients together and set aside. Cut the turkey meat and the celery into fine strips. Heat the oil in a pan to a fairly high temperature and in it quick fry the garlic, crushed, the onion, sliced and the ginger, until a light golden brown. Now add the turkey meat and quick fry for 7 to 10 minutes. Lift this mixture from the pan, pour a little more oil into it, heat through and then add the vegetables. Quick fry for 2 minutes, then return the turkey to this mixture, stir and add the ready-prepared sauce. Cook evenly for about a minute, then add the thickening, that is the cornflour dissolved in the water. Cook for a further 2 to 3 minutes when simmering point has been reached.

TURKEY CUTLETS

1 pound turkey meat	salt and pepper
2 ounces mushrooms	flour
½ cup milk	brown bread-crumbs
2 eggs	butter, margarine or oil (for
2 slices white bread	frying)

Mince the turkey and mushrooms together and season. Soak the bread in the milk, then squeeze and mix the bread with the turkey and mushrooms. Add one beaten egg yolk and shape the mixture into rissoles, either sausage-shaped or flattened. Flour them lightly, dip in beaten egg and brown bread-crumbs and fry in hot butter, margarine or cooking oil, for about 3 minutes each side, until nicely browned. Serve with vegetables or salad.

TURKEY HASH

1 pound cooked turkey meat	2 ounces butter or margarine
8 ounces cooked potatoes	6 to 8 rashers bacon
2 ounces mushrooms	sweet-corn kernels
a little chicken stock or turkey giblet stock	parsley
	seasoning

Sauté the mushrooms and then chop into fairly small pieces. Mix the turkey meat, diced, the cooked mushrooms, and the cooked potatoes, diced, with the parsley and seasoning. Add sufficient stock to make a not too moist mixture. Heat the butter in a pan and turn into it the turkey mixture. Smooth and flatten and cook over a moderate heat to brown underneath. Meanwhile make the bacon into rolls, place on skewers, and grill, turning frequently so that they become evenly crisp. Take from the grill and keep hot. Dribble a little melted butter over the pan mixture and place it under the hot grill so that the top becomes brown. Turn the hash on to a serving dish, garnish with the bacon rolls and with sweet-corn kernels, which meanwhile have been heated in a saucepan.

Cold Turkey Dishes

These dishes, like many given in the preceding section, are designed to make good use of left-over roast bird. Turkey meat can be substituted for the chicken meat which is called for in many of the recipes on pages 21 to 90. For example, Summer Mould, page 86; Chicken Mousse, page 86; Cream Mousse, page 88; Chicken Mould, page 85; Chicken and Ham Mousse, page 86; Chicken Loaf, page 84; Fruited Chicken Salad, page 82; Cold Chicken Soufflé, page 83; Roast Chicken Salad, page 83; Riviera Salad, page 80; Chicken and Rice Salad, page 78; Chicken Flan, page 89; Picnic Pasties, page 89. Further ways of using turkey meat are given in the following recipes.

TURKEY AND CHICORY SALAD

1 pound cooked chopped turkey
¼ pint whipped cream
2 tablespoons mayonnaise
pinch cayenne pepper
pinch black pepper

¼ teaspoon salt
2 heads chicory
2 or 3 tomatoes
half celery heart, chopped
3 to 4 inches cucumber

Combine the turkey with cream mixed with the mayonnaise, season with the cayenne, black pepper and salt. Chill well, then pile up in the centre of a circular platter. Cut the chicory in quarters. Arrange these around the dish. Put the sliced tomatoes, chopped celery and sliced cucumber between the pieces of chicory. Sprinkle with salt and pepper and serve extra mayonnaise separately.

BUFFET SALAD

1 pound diced cooked turkey
¼ cup French dressing
¼ cup diced green pepper or
     pimento
salt and pepper to taste
2 cups boiled rice

1 cup shredded celery
½ cup mayonnaise
cranberry jelly
lettuces as required
watercress and lemon juice

Mix turkey with rice and French dressing. Stand in a cold place until required. Just before serving, stir in celery, green pepper or pimento, mayonnaise, salt and pepper to taste, and lemon juice. Make cups with hearts of lettuce leaves on 8 plates. Spoon in salad. Garnish with cranberry jelly and arrange a ring of watercress around the base of each lettuce. This quantity makes 8 servings.

PARTY MOULDS

8 ounces cooked turkey
4 ounces mushrooms
¼ pint white sauce
½ pint aspic jelly
¼ pint milk

salt and pepper
green salad
tomatoes
cucumber
stuffed olives

Make the aspic jelly up as directed on the packet, and pour into individual moulds, setting in the top of each a piece of sliced, stuffed olive. Leave to cool. Meanwhile braise the mushrooms in the milk and when cooked, chop finely. Chop the turkey meat, mix with the mushrooms, season with salt and pepper, stir in the white sauce and the remainder of the aspic jelly. Pour into the moulds and leave to set. When required, turn out on to a bed of lettuce and garnish with sliced tomatoes and cucumber. These individual moulds are particularly suitable for parties, as they are easier to handle than the larger variety.

HAM AND TURKEY CREAMS

4 ounces ham
4 ounces cooked turkey
½ pint aspic jelly

¼ pint white sauce
½ ounce gelatine
1 tablespoon sherry

Make up the aspic jelly as instructed on the packet, and thinly coat 8 individual moulds. Mince the turkey and the ham separately and pound them until smooth. Now add half the sauce and half the sherry to each. Mix well and season. Blend half the aspic jelly into the ham mixture and divide between the 8 moulds. Now add the remaining jelly to the pounded turkey and top the moulds with the mixture. Leave to set and when required, dip the moulds in warm water briefly, wipe the outsides, and turn on to a serving platter. Serve with cooked cooled garden peas garnished with tomato wedges.

SPICED TURKEY LOAF

12 ounces cooked turkey meat
8 ounces pork sausage meat
1 medium onion

garlic salt
pepper
turkey stock

sprinkle of parsley
pinch of spice (mixed)
pinch nutmeg

½ pint aspic jelly
1 teaspoon sherry or brandy
2 bay leaves

Mince together the turkey meat, onion and parsley. In a bowl, mix this with the salt, pepper, spice and nutmeg and bind with the turkey stock. Grease a loaf tin and place half the turkey mixture in the pan, pressing it well down. Cover with half the sausage meat, then put in the remainder of the turkey mixture and finally the rest of the sausage meat. Place the 2 bay leaves on top and bake for 1 hour in a slow oven, 300° F (Gas 2).

Meanwhile, make up the aspic jelly according to the packet instructions, add the sherry or brandy, and when the loaf is quite cold, remove the bay leaves, turn it on to a dish and pour the jelly over. Leave to set in a cold place. Serve with the salad of your choice.

POTTED TURKEY

1 pound left-over turkey meat
3 ounces margarine
3 cooked bacon rashers or 3 ounces cooked ham or boiled bacon

salt and pepper
2 bay leaves

Pre-heat the oven at 275° F (Gas 1). Mince the turkey meat very finely and into it beat 2 ounces margarine. Season and spread in a fireproof dish, previously brushed with melted margarine. Place the bay leaves on the top and bake for 30 minutes on the middle shelf of the oven. Remove when cooked, cool and pour the remaining margarine, melted, over. Use as a savoury spread on toast, biscuits, etc. Keep in the refrigerator.

TURKEY BRAWN

4 pigs' trotters, cleaned
2 pounds veal bones, broken
1½ pounds cold turkey meat (or a mixture of turkey meat, ham, luncheon meat, etc.)

1 to 2 tablespoons tomato sauce
chopped parsley
salt and pepper

Wash the pigs' trotters well, and place them with the veal bones in a large saucepan. Fill almost to the top with cold water, add a little salt, bring to the boil. Boil for 5 minutes, skimming if necessary. Now lower the heat, cover and simmer gently for at least 3 hours until the meat falls from the bones. Remove from the heat, strain off the stock, reserve the meat and return the stock to the pan. Bring it to the boil again and boil it fast for about 30 minutes to reduce in quantity. Cut the meat into small dice, take the pan off the heat and stir the meat into the stock. Replace over the heat and simmer for 10 minutes, then remove again and stir in the tomato sauce and chopped parsley and season with salt and pepper to taste. Pour into wetted plain moulds or glass dishes, dividing the meat evenly. Leave to set. Before turning out, scrape off the fat from the top. Serve, sliced with salad and pickle.

Goose

If possible, get your goose ready-plucked and dressed. Unless a goose is plucked while it is still warm, it is quite hard work. In fact you have to undertake a kind of double operation because in addition to the outer layer of feathers which need to be plucked in the ordinary way, there is an under layer of down. Goose skin is tough, so you will not easily tear it, but there does seem to be a great deal of area to cover. Pluck the upper layer of feathers by taking two or three at a time and pulling them sharply in the direction of the head. For the under layer of down, roll it out with the ball of your thumb, picking it up between thumb and forefinger. Singe off the remaining fluff with a lighted taper or gas flame, being careful not to burn the flesh. Cut the wings off at the "elbow" joint to save having to pull out the pinions.

To remove the head, cut through the neck skin about two inches above the shoulders. Now draw the skin back and cut the neck as close to the body of the bird as you possibly can. To take off the feet, cut round the heel joint, break the bone and remove the paddles and draw the tendons as for other birds. These tendons are quite hard to draw out; there are about six in each leg and each needs to be pulled out singly.

To draw the bird, open it down from the breast bone to the vent. In the resulting hole, insert your fingers and take hold of the gizzard, entrails, lungs, windpipe and gullet, and any fat that you can draw out. Keep the giblets (that is the heart, gizzard and liver) and, of course, the fat, and then discard the remaining entrails. Taking great care, as when drawing other birds, not to puncture the gall-bladder. Having made sure that the bird is empty and clean, wipe it thoroughly with a clean, damp cloth.

After stuffing the bird (see below), truss it ready for roasting. Tuck the tail into the vent end and secure it with a small skewer. Pass other skewers through the body in two or three places and then wind string round the skewers to keep them in position. Do not pass the string over the breast of the goose. Tuck the neck skin in under the string.

If using oven-ready frozen goose, read the important note on thawing poultry on page 17.

Stuffings for Roast Goose

As goose, like duck, possesses a great deal of fat, most of the stuffings suggested for duck are equally suitable for goose, but remember that the goose has a very large cavity and therefore it will be necessary to make at least double the quantity.

SAGE AND ONION STUFFING

4 ounces bread-crumbs
4 onions
1 dessertspoon powdered sage
1 ounce butter

1 egg
pepper and salt
stock or water

Simmer the onions, peeled and finely chopped in a little water or stock until tender. Add the sage, bread-crumbs, butter, seasoning and mix well. Then add sufficient beaten egg to bind into a firm stuffing.

CELERY AND APPLE STUFFING

3 ounces bread-crumbs
2 onions
2 to 3 ounces bacon
4 to 5 tablespoons chopped celery

4 medium-sized cooking apples
1½ tablespoons chopped parsley
salt and pepper

Dice the bacon and brown it in its own fat. Lift from the pan and in the residual fat gently cook the chopped onions and celery. Cook for 5 minutes and remove. Still using the same fat, fry the apples, diced, until they are tender and brown. Now mix these cooked ingredients together with the bread-crumbs, herbs, seasoning and use to stuff the bird.

TANGERINE AND CHESTNUT STUFFING

2 ounces butter
½ cup diced celery (with some leaves)
3 tangerines
1 cup cooked, chopped chestnuts

2 cups cooked rice
8 ounce packet sage and onion stuffing mix
½ cup stock or water

116

Melt the butter in a pan and in it cook the celery over a medium heat for about 8 minutes. Peel the tangerines, remove the white membranes. Cut the sections into halves and take out the pips. Mix together the tangerines, stuffing mix, chestnuts, seasonings, rice and stock, then add the cooked celery and butter, and mix together lightly with a fork. Add a little more stock if necessary.

APPLE AND POTATO STUFFING

8 ounces mashed potato (dry)
2 large cooking apples
2 medium-sized onions
½ teaspoon powdered sage
1 level teaspoon thyme (powdered)
salt and pepper

Chop the apples and mix with the powdered herbs. Parboil the onions, chop and add to all the other ingredients. Season to taste. Bind with a little beaten egg or milk.

PRUNE AND RAISIN STUFFING

1 pound prunes
3 tablespoons raisins
4 large cooking apples
1 level teaspoon salt
¼ teaspoon pepper
1 egg

Soak the prunes for at least 2 hours, covering with boiling water, then stone and chop them and mix with the apples, peeled, cored and chopped, and the raisins, rinsed. Add the seasoning and bind with the egg, well beaten.

APRICOT STUFFING

Especially suitable for roast wild goose.

2 ounces butter
2 ounces chopped onion
1 cup chopped cooking apple
1 cup chopped dried apricots
3 cups soft white bread-crumbs
½ teaspoon salt
good pinch pepper

In a large saucepan, melt the butter and in it cook the onion until tender. Now stir in the chopped apple and apricots, the bread-crumbs, salt and pepper, and mix thoroughly together.

WALNUT STUFFING

4 ounces bread-crumbs	2 large cooking apples
1 teaspoon powdered mixed herbs	4 ounces pork sausage meat
2 dozen walnuts	
2 medium onions	1 egg
1 ounce butter	a little milk

Chop the onions finely and fry till soft and pale gold in the melted butter. Peel the apples and walnuts, chop both and mix all the ingredients together. Bind with the beaten egg and add as much milk as necessary to form a firm yet manageable stuffing.

Roast Goose Dishes

Roasting is by far the best way of cooking goose, and variety can be supplied from time to time by using different stuffings. The foregoing recipes giving various stuffings will indicate how this can be done. Below is the basic roasting method followed by a few variations, using particular stuffings for particular effect.

ROAST GOOSE

Sprinkle the prepared and stuffed bird with salt and place on a trivet in a roasting pan, on its side. Place on the bird a little of the fat reserved from drawing or about 2 tablespoons of melted butter or margarine. Goose makes its own fat for cooking, so no more than this is necessary. Cover with foil and roast at 400° F (Gas 6) for the first hour, then turn the bird on its other side, baste well, and lower the heat to 375° F (Gas 5). Allow 15 to 18 minutes per pound and baste frequently for the rest of the cooking time. Turn the bird with breast uppermost for the last 30 minutes and remove the foil so that the breast will become nicely browned. Spoon off some of the excess fat when you are basting and reserve in a basin. If the pan tends to get a little too brown, add half a cup of hot water to the juices.

An alternative method of cooking is to roast in a moderate oven 350° F (Gas 4) throughout, allowing 25 to 30 minutes per pound. Remove the foil for the last half hour as above. When the bird is cooked, the legs should move up and down quite freely. To confirm that it is ready, cut a leg free, press it out and down, and if the hip joint dislocates easily the bird is cooked.

Pour off the goose-grease into a bowl. Scatter a tablespoon of flour into the remaining juices in the pan, stir thoroughly and put back over the heat. Pour in stock made from the giblets which have previously been simmered. Boil the gravy until smooth. Serve with apple sauce.

APPLE SAUCE

1½ pounds cooking apples	2 ounces sugar
2 medium onions	4 cloves
2 ounces butter	1 tablespoon cooking sherry

Chop the onion very finely, peel, core and chop the apples. Melt the butter in a saucepan and in it cook the onion until it begins to go transparent. Then add the apple. Sprinkle over the sugar, stir constantly, and cook slowly until the apple softens. Add the cloves and finally the cooking sherry, a tablespoon or more if liked.

DANISH ROAST GOOSE

1 goose	1 teaspoon sugar per cup of
salt	stuffing
prunes	red-currant jelly
cooking apples	

The amount of stuffing used will depend on the size of the goose. Allow for each pound of the bird, ready-to-cook weight, one cup of mixed apples and prunes. Soak the prunes for at least 2 hours, then drain and take out the stones. Peel, core and slice the apples, mix together and sprinkle with the sugar. Sprinkle the inside of the goose cavity with salt, then fill with the prepared fruit. Truss and roast as above. Into the final gravy stir a tablespoon of red-currant jelly (or 2 tablespoons).

GOOSE WITH RED CABBAGE

1 goose	salt
2 pounds cooking apples	pinch cinnamon
12 ounces sultanas and	a little butter
currants (mixed)	1 medium red cabbage
4 ounces fine bread-crumbs	6 smoked sausages
2 eggs	3 tablespoons vinegar

Make a stuffing by mixing the apples, peeled, cored and cut into pieces, with the fruit, bread-crumbs, cinnamon, salt and eggs, well beaten. Place this stuffing into the prepared bird, and place it on a trivet in a baking tin. Add ½ pint of water to the tin and spread a little butter over the bird. Roast in the usual way (see page 118), basting frequently.

Meanwhile shred the cabbage, wash and dry it, and then simmer in a very little stock until almost tender. Now add the sausages, cut into pieces, and when the cabbage is quite soft, stir in the vinegar. When the goose is cooked, serve on a dish with the cabbage and sausages and accompanied with boiled or sautéed potatoes. For the gravy, pour off the goose fat and stir the liquid from the cabbage into the remaining drippings. Bring to the boil, strain and serve.

RUSSIAN ROAST GOOSE

1 goose	1 medium head celery
½ teaspoon carraway seeds	3 to 4 onions
2 pounds cooking apples	salt

Rub the prepared bird with salt, inside and out. Sprinkle the carraway seeds into the cavity, then stuff with the apples left whole, the celery and onions, cleaned and chopped. Roast in the usual way (see page 118).

GIBLET PIE

1 set goose giblets	salt and pepper
1 pound good quality braising steak	puff or shortcrust pastry
	milk for glazing
1 onion	bouquet garni

Place the washed giblets in a saucepan together with the onion, sliced, the bouquet garni and seasonings, and cover with cold water. Simmer on a low heat for about 2 hours. Leave to cool. Meanwhile mince the steak or cut it very finely, season, and when the giblets are cool, place alternate layers of meat and chopped giblets in a pie-dish which should be just large enough to take the quantity. Strain the giblet stock and put into the dish until about three-quarters full. Make puff or short pastry based on 6 ounces flour, roll out, cover the pie-dish, glaze with a little milk, and bake in a hot oven 425° F (Gas 7) for 20 minutes, then lower the heat to 350° F (Gas 4) and continue cooking for about a further 50 minutes. Use the remaining goose giblet stock to make a gravy.

GOOSE LIVER PÂTÉ

6 ounces goose liver	bouquet garni
3 ounces butter	salt
1 small onion	freshly-ground black pepper
$\frac{1}{8}$ teaspoon grated nutmeg	1 dessertspoon brandy

Melt 1 ounce of butter in a saucepan and in it fry the onion, very finely chopped, until it begins to turn golden brown. Now add the goose liver, herbs, a little salt, pepper, nutmeg and fry slowly for 4 minutes, turning once. Leave to cool, then pass twice through a mincer and finally through a fine sieve. Cream the remaining butter, work it into the liver mixture, and finally add the brandy. Pack the pâté into a china jar and seal with clarified butter. Keep in a refrigerator, but not for more than a few days.

Duck

Duck (or duckling) should be eaten before it is 12 months old. After that it is liable to be tough. When buying a non-prepared bird, watch out for bright yellow feet and a bill which is soft enough to bend back easily. The breast flesh should be white and meaty. To dress, follow the instructions as for chicken on page 18.

Before cooking a frozen (oven-ready) bird, make sure that it is *completely thawed out*—5 to 8 hours, or preferably left overnight. If it is necessary to thaw the bird quickly, submerge it (wrapped) in cold water for about 2 hours. (See note on washing frozen poultry, page 19.)

ROAST DUCK

Pre-heat your oven to 350° F (Gas 4). Remove the giblets and use them for making stock. Rinse the duckling, dry, and stuff in whatever way you choose. Alternatively, insert into the cavity one whole washed orange. Always stuff the duck from the vent end. Brush the bird with oil or melted butter and cook in a roasting tin, allowing 30 minutes to the pound. As duck carries a good deal of fat, it is not necessary to baste.

Stuffings for Roast Duck

APPLE AND CELERY STUFFING

2 ounces bacon or salt pork	3 ounces white bread-crumbs
2 onions	2 tablespoons chopped parsley
2 large sticks celery	salt and pepper
4 medium cooking apples	a little sugar to taste

Rind the bacon, chop it (or the salt pork) and place in a stout frying-pan to draw off the fat. Cook the bacon or pork in its own fat for about 3 minutes until brown, then lift with a slotted spoon and reserve. Skin and chop the onions, fry in the pork fat together with the celery, scrubbed and chopped, for about 5 minutes; then remove from the pan. Meanwhile peel and dice the apples, now add them to the same fat and fry until tender and brown. Mix all these ingredients and the crumbs and seasonings together, adding a little melted butter to bind if necessary.

ORANGE AND HERB STUFFING

4 tablespoons white bread-crumbs

2 tablespoons chopped herbs (parsley, thyme, chives, marjoram)

2 tablespoons onion (finely chopped)

1 to 1½ ounces butter

juice and grated rind of 1 large orange

1 egg

salt and pepper

Mix in a bowl the crumbs, herbs and seasoning. Melt the butter in a pan and in it soften the onion, but do not let it brown. Add the cooked onion to the herb mixture, together with the grated orange rind and juice. Bind with the egg, well beaten, and if the mixture is still too dry and crumbly, add a little extra orange juice.

CRANBERRY STUFFING

½ pound fresh white bread-crumbs

¾ pound prunes, pre-soaked

2 large apples, peeled and diced

3 ounces almonds, blanched and chopped

4 tablespoons whole berry cranberry sauce

grated rind and juice of 1 lemon

2 eggs

2 tablespoons corn oil

Place bread-crumbs in a bowl. Add the roughly chopped prunes, apple, almonds, cranberry sauce and lemon. Bind together with the beaten eggs and corn oil.

ORANGE APRICOT STUFFING

3 dessertspoons corn oil

1 medium onion

3 or 4 celery stalks and leaves

2 ounces mushrooms

2 oranges

8 ounces dried apricots

3 cups ready-cooked rice (preferably brown)

½ teaspoon salt

½ teaspoon thyme

pinch of cinnamon

pinch of mace

Chop the onion and the celery finely, heat the oil and in it sauté the onion, celery and the mushrooms, thinly sliced. Grate the rind from the two oranges and squeeze the juice to make up to one cupful. Chop the dried apricots finely and mix together with all the other ingredients. Add the seasonings and spices and the ready-cooked rice. Mix all ingredients thoroughly together.

SWEDISH STUFFING

2 cups ready-cooked rice
½ cup sultanas or seedless raisins
pinch ground cardamom
1 piece onion

1 teaspoon grated orange rind
½ teaspoon salt
2 dessertspoons melted butter
1 apple

Peel and grate the apple, chop the onion very finely. Wash and drain the sultanas or raisins and mix together with the ready-cooked rice, orange rind, onion, melted butter, apple and seasonings. Blend all ingredients lightly with a fork, and stuff into the body cavity of the duck.

Roast Duck Dishes

ROAST DUCKLING WITH APPLE AND ONION SAUCE

1 duckling
1 peeled onion or sage and onion
   stuffing

salt and pepper to taste
1 ounce softened butter or
   dripping

Prepare a moderately slow oven, 325° F (Gas 3). Remove giblets from the body cavity of the thawed duck and wipe with a damp cloth (see note about washing poultry, p. 19). Season inside and out with salt and pepper. Spread the bird all over with softened butter or dripping. Insert into body cavity the stuffing or peeled onion and the liver. Place in shallow roasting tin. Cook, allowing 30 minutes per pound. Drain off surplus fat and make gravy with giblet stock. Serve with apple and onion sauce, orange salad, green peas or braised celery.

Apple and onion sauce
1 pound apples
2 tablespoons sherry or water
1 tablespoon chopped onion

½ ounce butter
1 tablespoon brown or caster
   sugar

Peel, core and slice the apples, thinly. Place in a saucepan with the sherry or water and chopped onion. Cover closely. Simmer gently, stirring occasionally till into a pulp. Add butter and sugar. Stir till butter and sugar are melted. Serve in a heated sauce-boat.

ROAST DUCK A L'ORANGE

1 duck
2 large oranges
2 level teaspoons arrowroot
¾ pint stock (made from bird giblets)

3 teaspoons sherry
2 teaspoons lemon juice

Roast the duck at 350° F (Gas 4) allowing 30 minutes per pound, or at 400° F (Gas 6) allowing 20 minutes per pound. Meanwhile wash the oranges, peel off the thin outer skins and blanch in boiling water. Cut the skin into very thin strips. Mix a little cold stock into the arrowroot, then boil the remainder and stir in the blended arrowroot, cooking for 3 minutes and stirring all the time. Add the lemon juice and juice of the two peeled oranges. Next add the sherry and finally the shredded orange peel. Place the cooked duck on a serving dish and pour over it this orange sauce. Serve with vegetables and, if possible, an orange salad made from oranges skinned and thinly sliced and sprinkled with chopped mint and French dressing.

DUCK WITH GOOSEBERRY SAUCE

1 duck
½ pint gooseberry purée
1 tablespoon sugar

a little butter
1 teaspoon lemon juice
1 wine glass sherry

Roast the duck towards the top of the oven until tender. Baste it about every 15 or 20 minutes with the fat that runs out. Meanwhile mix together the gooseberry purée, sugar, lemon juice and butter (about a tablespoonful), and heat slowly.

Just before you are ready to serve, add the sherry to this sauce. Do not pour it over the bird, but pass it separately.

CRANBERRY DUCKLING

1 duck (5 to 6 pounds)
cranberry stuffing (see page 126)
½ ounce cornflour
4 ounces sugar

1 pound fresh cranberries
¼ pint water
¼ pint orange juice
1 orange

Stuff the duck with the cranberry stuffing and roast until almost tender and the skin is a light brown. Meanwhile, make the sauce by placing the water, sugar, cranberries, cornflour and orange juice in a saucepan. Bring it to the boil, stirring constantly, and cook over a medium heat until the liquid is clear and syrupy (about 5 minutes). Remove from the heat and add the orange which is unpeeled but cut into thick wedges (about 6). Remove the duck from the oven and transfer it to a deep casserole. Pour the sauce over the bird, cover, and return to the oven for about a further 20 minutes, or until the duck feels tender when pricked. Baste the duck once during this cooking period.

NORWEGIAN PRUNE-STUFFED DUCK

1 duck (4 to 5 pounds)
pepper
salt
5 apples
15 prunes

3 tablespoons flour
1 gill cream
¾ pint giblet gravy
a little black-currant juice

Season and prepare the duck for roasting in the usual way. Stuff the apples, peeled and sliced, and the prunes into the vent end. Sew the bird up and roast until crisp and tender. Place on a serving dish when cooked, pour off the gravy and skim the fat from it. Now add a little water and stir in the flour to thicken. Next add the giblet gravy, cream and a little black-currant juice (optional). Serve the bird with baked or fried potatoes and with more cooked prunes and apples if you wish. Serve the sauce separately.

DUCKLING WITH LIVER STUFFING

1 duckling
cooking fat

¾ pint brown sauce
1 orange

Stuffing

1 chicken liver
1 duckling liver
½ teaspoon parsley
¼ teaspoon thyme
1 ounce butter

1 egg
pinch nutmeg
salt and pepper
3 ounces white bread-crumbs

Pour boiling water over the two livers to blanch them, then chop finely, adding the herbs, seasoning, nutmeg, bread-crumbs and melted butter. Bind with the lightly beaten egg and stuff the duckling with the liver mixture. Truss the bird, baste well with hot fat, and place in a hot oven, 425° F (Gas 7). Cook for 30 minutes, basting twice. Then drain off the fat, pour the brown sauce (hot) into the baking tin and continue cooking until the duckling is tender, basting the bird frequently with the sauce.

Peel and section the orange, place it in a basin with some wine or stock, and heat it over a pan of hot water. When the bird is ready, place on a serving dish, strain a little of the sauce round the bird, and garnish with the hot orange. Pour the rest of the sauce in a sauce-boat to pass separately. (See Brown Sauce recipe below.)

BROWN SAUCE

1 small carrot
1 onion
1 ounce dripping

1 ounce flour
1 pint good stock
salt and pepper

Melt the dripping and in it gently fry the onion and carrot, thinly sliced, until golden brown. Stir in the flour, lower the heat, fry very slowly until the flour too is brown. Then add the stock, bring to simmering point, season, and simmer for 25 minutes. Strain the stock before using. If the colour is not quite deep enough for your taste, you may add a little gravy browning or meat or vegetable extract to add depth of colour as well as an extra flavour.

PORTUGUESE DUCK

1 duck (about 5 pounds)
1 cup port wine
salt and pepper

celery stalks or vine leaves *or*
1 apple, 1 slice onion,
2 celery stalks

Wipe the duck inside and out with a damp cloth. Season the cavity with salt and pepper, and in it place some scrubbed celery stalks, or vine leaves or an apple, quartered but unpeeled, a slice of onion and 2 celery stalks. (Remove these items once the bird is cooked.) Truss the bird if required and then prick the skin on the fatty back layer and around legs and wings with a sharp fork. Do not dig the fork too deeply into the bird or the fat will tend to run into the bird instead of running out. Place the bird, breast side up, on a wire rack in a baking tin. Pour about $\frac{1}{2}$ cup of port wine into the tin, and place the tin in the oven, 350° F (Gas 4). Cook, allowing about 30 minutes per pound, basting frequently with the wine and the drippings from the bird, adding more wine as required, or until you have used up the entire cupful. The skin of the bird should be brown and crisp by the time it is tender. Dish and serve with roast or French-fried potatoes and green peas. Strain the gravy from the dripping and wine and pass separately in a sauce-boat.

CHINESE ROAST DUCK

1 plump duck	4 spring onions (optional)
2 tablespoons brandy or sherry	salt
1½ dessertspoons soy sauce	3 teaspoons Worcester sauce
1 clove garlic (crushed)	2 tablespoons honey
	1 cup hot water

Mix together the brandy or sherry, soy sauce, crushed garlic, chopped spring onions, Worcester sauce and salt. Pour this mixture into the duck's cavity and rub well in. Seal the opening and wipe the duck dry on the outside. Mix together the honey and water and pour this over the duck a number of times (at least 8 times). Leave until dry and then repeat the process. The honey will give colour and crispness to the skin.

Meanwhile heat the oven to 375° F (Gas 5) and roast the duck breast upwards on a grid in a shallow roasting tin. Turn the bird in about 20 minutes when it has become a rich reddish brown and cook for a further 20 minutes. Brush with the drippings from time to time, turn the bird breast side uppermost again, and cook till tender and well browned. Place on a serving dish, reduce the gravy from the pan and serve it with the bird.

An alternative method is to omit the savoury mixture for the cavity and simply glaze the bird with the honey and warm water. (In this case reduce water to ¾ cup.) Leave it to stand for 2 to 3 hours so that the honey glaze will be absorbed, and then roast on a spit or rotisserie. Serve the duck cut into small pieces with the crisp skin cut into crackling strips.

CANETON NANTAIS

1 duck (3 pounds)	3 to 4 rashers streaky bacon, quartered
2 ounces margarine	¾ pint stock
4 medium onions, quartered	8 ounce packet peas, just thawed

Pre-heat the oven at 375° F (Gas 5). Remove the giblets from the duckling and simmer in a little water to make the stock. Melt the margarine in a roasting tin and cook the duck for 30 minutes. Remove the duck from the roasting tin and place in a deep casserole, add the onion, bacon and stock. Cover and cook for another 30 minutes. Add the peas to the casserole and continue cooking for a further 15 minutes or until the duck is tender. Serve on a large dish with the vegetables and stock spooned round.

DUCK WITH PEACHES

1 duck	$\frac{1}{2}$ cup vermouth
1 tablespoon sugar	6 peaches
2 ounces butter	salt and pepper
$\frac{1}{2}$ cup stock	

Peel, halve and stone the peaches. Sprinkle them with vermouth and set aside. Melt the butter in a roasting dish and brown the duck well in it all over, sprinkling it with sugar as you brown it. Pour in the stock, add seasoning. Cover with foil, and cook in the oven until tender. Remove the covering for the last 20 minutes of cooking to brown the breast. When cooked, place the duck on a heated serving dish and keep it hot. Spoon off the fat from the pan in which the duck has been cooked. Place in the remaining gravy the peach halves and the rest of the vermouth. Leave to simmer for 2 to 3 minutes, garnish with the peach halves and pour sauce over the bird.

DUCK WITH RED CABBAGE

1 duck	$\frac{1}{2}$ pint red wine
1 red cabbage (medium)	2 tablespoons lemon juice
1 onion	$\frac{1}{2}$ teaspoon sugar
3 tablespoons butter	salt and pepper

Rub the duck with salt both inside and out. Roast in a moderate oven for 1 hour, then remove it from the pan and keep it hot, draining off the excess fat from the pan juices. Meanwhile shred the cabbage, sprinkle with salt and leave for about 15 minutes until it makes its liquid. Squeeze out this liquid and drain the cabbage thoroughly. Chop the onion and fry it until soft in the heated butter. Add the drained cabbage, stir thoroughly together and cook for 2 to 3 minutes, then add the wine, sugar, the seasoning and the lemon juice. Cover the pan and cook over a low heat for about 20 minutes. Now transfer the cabbage mixture to your roasting pan and place the duck on top of it. Cook the bird in the oven for about a further hour, or until it is tender.

DUCK WITH APRICOTS

1 duck (3 to 4 pounds)	3 tablespoons apricot brandy
1 dessertspoon honey	3 level teaspoons cornflour
1 tin apricot halves	1 teaspoon lemon juice
(medium size)	butter

Prepare and roast the duck in a moderate oven, but after it has been cooking for about 50 minutes, remove it from the oven and prick it very lightly to allow surplus fat to run out. Now brush the bird with a little warm honey, so as to give it a crisp brown skin, and put it back in the oven to finish cooking.

Meanwhile, make the sauce. Strain the liquid from the apricots and to it add the juice of the lemon and enough water to make up a total quantity of just under ½ pint. Blend in the cornflour, pour into a saucepan and cook until the sauce is smooth, thick and clear. Check the flavour and add a little sugar or honey if it is not sweet enough. Stir in a spoonful of butter to impart a shine to the sauce. Place the apricot halves in the sauce, heat through for a few moments, and then stir in the apricot brandy. Be careful not to let the sauce boil. Now remove the bird from the oven, place it on a heated serving dish, either whole or carved into joints. Top with the sauce and apricots, and garnish with a few sprigs of watercress.

ROAST DUCK WITH CHERRIES

1 duck (4½ to 5 pounds)	8 ounces streaky bacon rashers
1 tin cherries (16 ounces)	2 level tablespoons flour
3 tablespoons Italian	1 teaspoon sugar
vermouth	2 tablespoons fat

Place the fat in a roasting pan and pre-heat the oven to 400° F (Gas 6). Stuff the duck with the forcemeat of your choice, retruss and place it in the roasting pan. Tip the cherries into a bowl and stir in the vermouth. Wet the duck all over with the mixture, then cover the breast with about 4 bacon rashers. Sprinkle flour and sugar in the pan and bake for 10 minutes. Now reduce the heat to 325° F (Gas 3) and cook for a further 1½ hours or until the bird is tender.

Meanwhile boil the giblets in about ½ pint water for 30 minutes and make bacon rolls with the remaining streaky bacon by removing their rinds and rolling them up and baking on a fireproof plate in the oven for about ¼ hour. When the duck is ready, place on a heated serving dish. Spoon off as much of the fat from the pan as possible. Pour the giblet broth and the cherry and vermouth syrup into the pan, add salt and pepper and cook until the sauce is smooth and thick. Garnish the bird with cherries and bacon rolls and pour the sauce around the dish.

SPICED MALAY DUCK

1 duck (about 3 pounds)	$\frac{1}{2}$ tablespoon salt
1 cup plus 3 tablespoons thick coconut milk (see below)	1 dessertspoon sugar
1 tablespoon vinegar	2 hard-boiled eggs

For the paste

2$\frac{1}{2}$ tablespoons anise seeds	2 inches ginger root
$\frac{1}{2}$ tablespoon cumin seeds	$\frac{1}{4}$ pound shallots
5 tablespoons coriander seeds	2 cloves garlic
piece turmeric ($\frac{3}{4}$ inch)	

Onion mixture

2 ounces shallots	2 medium onions
2 fresh chillies, seeded (a quarter green pepper may be used instead for a milder flavour)	

Grind together and mix to a thick paste the ingredients for the paste and set aside a dessertspoon of this mixture. Slice the onion mixture ingredients finely. Now finely chop the heart, liver and gizzard of the bird and mix them with the cup of coconut milk, the sliced onion mixture, the ground spice mixture, the vinegar, salt and sugar. Cook this mixture over a medium heat for about 15 minutes and then stuff it into the vent end of the duck, with the hard-boiled eggs (whole). Now mix the three tablespoons of coconut milk with the reserved dessertspoon of ground spices and smear this over the bird. Grill the duck on a barbecue, or on a rotisserie, over direct heat or under a grill, placing it about 4 inches from the heat. Turn the bird frequently, dabbing it with the spicy paste until it forms a coating. This is rather a slow method of cooking duck, but the result is delicious.

To make coconut milk

Pour tepid water (about $\frac{1}{2}$ to $\frac{3}{4}$ cup per nut) on to coarsely grated coconut flesh. Leave 10 minutes, then squeeze well and strain through a fine nylon sieve.

PEKING DUCK

1 duckling   boiling water

For the sauce

1 cup soy sauce   good pinch pepper
½ cup sherry   3 spring onions, finely chopped
6 dessertspoons brown sugar   2 cloves garlic, crushed
1 dessertspoon salt

This is a traditional Chinese dish, which calls for a double cooking method of simmering and deep frying, to produce a bird which is crisp on the outside and tender on the inside. It does, however, have to be spread over two days.

First day. Mix the ingredients for the sauce, and place the sauce together with the duck in a deep vessel. Pour on enough boiling water almost to cover the bird, then cover it tightly with a lid or foil and simmer it until almost done, about 60 minutes. Lift the duck from the liquid and hang it to dry overnight. This can be done by tying the duck by the neck to the top rack in the oven, removing all other racks, and putting a foil-lined dish underneath. Before completing the dish next day, be sure that the duck is thoroughly dry or the dish will not be successful.

When ready to prepare the duck for the meal, heat about three inches of oil to 375° F (Gas 5) and brown the duck on both sides, which will only take a very few minutes. Carve and serve.

DUCK IN BEER

1 duck   salt and pepper
3 ounces butter   bouquet garni (2 sprigs parsley,
1 onion   1 sprig each thyme,
½ pint beer   marjoram, 1 bay leaf)
1 pound seedless grapes

Melt the butter in a casserole and in it brown the onion, finely chopped, and the duck. When the duck is brown on all sides, pour in the beer, add the bouquet garni and seasoning. Cover and cook until tender, basting with the juices from time to time. Test for tenderness after about an hour. When the duck is done, take it from the pan and keep it hot. Remove the bouquet garni from the pan juices, strain off as much fat as possible, then add the grapes and simmer them in the gravy for a few moments. Meanwhile cut the duck into portions. Arrange on the serving-dish, and when the sauce is ready, pour it and the grapes over the portions and serve.

BRAISED DUCKLING

1 duckling	1½ ounces flour
a little hot fat	1 pint stock
2 onions	2 sage leaves
2 ounces butter	sprig of thyme

Baste the trussed duck with hot fat and place to cook in a hot oven, 425° F (Gas 7) until well browned. Baste the bird every few minutes. Meantime, slice the onions finely, and fry them in the butter until golden brown. Remove the onions from the fat and stir into it the flour, cooking until that too is brown. Remove the duck from the oven, place in a large saucepan, pour enough stock over it almost to cover the bird, then add the fried onions, seasoning and herbs, and cover with a closely-fitting lid. Simmer gently until tender (45 to 60 minutes). When the duck is cooked, strain the sauce from the pan, and stir about ¾ of a pint of it into your brown roux. Bring to the boil, stirring, and cook for 5 minutes. Taste for seasoning and adjust as necessary. Serve the duck with the gravy and with buttered green peas.

BRAISED DUCK AND PINEAPPLE

1 duckling	½ pint brown sauce (see page 130)
1 small tin pineapple chunks	1 teaspoon tomato ketchup
½ pint inexpensive white wine	a little dripping

Drain the pineapple, place the chunks in the wine and leave to soak for several hours. When ready to cook the dish, place the duck in dripping in your oven for about 40 minutes (325° F, Gas 3), and then drain off all the fat. Drain the pineapple, mix the liquid with the brown sauce and tomato ketchup, and pour it over the duck. Cover the dish with a closely-fitting lid or aluminium foil and put it back in the oven for a further hour, at 375° F (Gas 5). Just before you are ready to serve, place the pineapple pieces in a saucepan to heat through. Put the duck on a hot dish and garnish with the pineapple, then pour the sauce over the bird, either whole or already carved.

LUXURY DUCK À L'ORANGE

1 tender duckling, ready pre- pared (5 to 6 pounds)	1 tablespoon white wine vinegar
salt and pepper	5 oranges
6 tablespoons corn oil	2 tablespoons cranberry with orange relish
¼ pint Cointreau	¼ pint beef stock
1 tablespoon sugar	watercress for garnish

Joint the duck. Heat the corn oil in a casserole and sauté the duck until evenly browned. Reduce the heat, cover and simmer gently till tender, turning from time to time. Add two-thirds of the Cointreau and simmer for 5 minutes. Remove the duck and keep hot. Add the vinegar, sugar, juice of 1 orange, cranberry and orange relish and beef stock. Bring to the boil, stirring all the time. Reduce the heat and simmer gently for 10 minutes. Skim the fat from the surface and strain the sauce. Season according to taste and add remaining Cointreau. Peel and segment the remaining oranges. Place half of them in the sauce and bring to the boil. Place duck on a serving-dish, pour a little sauce around the duck. Garnish with remaining orange segments and water-cress. Serve the remaining sauce separately.

DUCK WITH OLIVES

1 duckling	3 dozen olives
1 pint beef stock	salt and pepper
2 onions	

Joint the duck, season and place in a casserole. Chop the onions, the duck's liver, gizzard and heart and a dozen stoned olives. Place this mixture on the joints and cover with the hot stock. Simmer for 1 hour to 1¼ hours, gently, until the duck is tender. Just before you are ready to serve, place the remaining olives in the casserole for a few minutes. When the duck is cooked, lift the pieces on to a hot serving-dish and pour over it the sauce, garnished with the olives.

CHINESE SAVOURY DUCK

1 duck, about 3 pounds	3 dessertspoons frying oil
2 cups water	1 medium onion
1 dessertspoon cornflour	1 clove garlic
2 dessertspoons water	1 or 2 thin slices ginger

For sauce

1 cup soy sauce	2 dessertspoons brown sugar
2 dessertspoons dry sherry	1 scant teaspoon salt

Heat the oil in a deep frying-pan to about 350° F (Gas 4). Quickly fry the duck cut into 6 or 8 pieces until golden brown. Drain off the excess oil, then add the onions, garlic and ginger and fry with the duck for a further 2 minutes. Meanwhile, mix the sauce ingredients together and add the sauce to the duck in the pan. Mix well, then pour over two cups water and bring to the boil. Cover the pan and leave to simmer gently for about 2 hours. Just before you are ready to serve, add the cornflour moistened with 2 dessertspoons of water, to thicken the sauce. Stir and cook for a further 2 minutes before serving.

SAVOURY DUCK WITH CHESTNUTS

1 duck (3 pounds)
2 cups water
1 pound chestnuts

condiments and sauce as for Chinese Savoury Duck (page 137)

Place the chestnuts in boiling water in a deep pan and boil for 30 minutes. Cool and shell the chestnuts. Meanwhile cook the duck as for Savoury Duck (page 137), and simmer for 1½ hours, covered. Now add the chestnuts and cook, covered, for a further 30 minutes on a low heat.

DUCK WITH YOUNG TURNIPS

1 duckling
2 ounces butter
1 pound young turnips
pinch thyme
2 teaspoons chopped parsley

salt and pepper
1 small onion
½ cup dry white wine or stock, or a mixture of both

Melt half the butter in a pan and in it brown the duck, cut into joints, together with the onion, chopped finely. Next add the wine or stock, seasonings and herbs, cover and cook on a low gas for 50 to 60 minutes. Meanwhile, boil the turnips in salted water until just tender, then drain and sauté them lightly in the remaining butter, making sure that they do not brown. The turnips can then either be added to the pan and cooked for a few minutes with the duckling, or they can be piled on to a serving-dish, sprinkled with chopped parsley and with the duckling joints arranged around them, and the sauce from the casserole poured over.

CASSOULET OF DUCK

1 duck (about 4 pounds)
3 onions
1 pound carrots
1 large can tomatoes
　　(1 pound 12 ounces)

2 cloves garlic, crushed
¼ teaspoon mixed herbs
1 teaspoon finely grated orange rind
salt and pepper

Wipe the duck with a clean, damp cloth, and cut into joints. Peel and chop the onions and carrots and place in a large casserole, with the tomatoes, garlic, herbs, orange rind and seasoning. Place the duck joints, skin side uppermost, on top of these ingredients, cover with a lid or foil and bake at 325° F (Gas 3) for 2 hours. Take the lid off for the last 20 minutes of cooking time and raise the heat to 400° F (Gas 6) in order to brown the duck. Before serving, skim off as much of the excess fat as possible. This makes a quantity sufficient for at least 6 servings.

CASSEROLED DUCK WITH RICE

1 duck	½ pint stock
2 onions	salt and pepper
3 carrots	a little fat
1 tablespoon chopped parsley	¼ pound Portuguese sausage
8 ounces long grain rice	

Joint the duck, chop the onions, slice the carrots and place them, together with the parsley and seasoning, in an ovenproof casserole. Pour on the stock, cover, and cook for about 1½ hours at 350° F (Gas 4). Next, drain off the stock, replace the casserole in the warm oven. Make up the stock to ¾ pint using water or other stock, and place it in a pan together with the rice. Bring to the boil, cover, simmer for about 15 minutes, or until the rice is tender and the liquid has been absorbed. Take care not to let the mixture get too dry, adding a little more liquid if necessary.

Meanwhile slice the sausage and fry in a little hot fat until well brown. Place half the rice on a serving dish, arrange on it the duckling joints, cover with the remaining rice and garnish with the sausage pieces.

FLORENTINE DUCK

1 young duckling (jointed)	salt and pepper
1 pound tomatoes	1 ounce butter
¼ pint red wine	2 ounces papper-delle (flat
½ teaspoon mixed herbs	macaroni)

Chop the tomatoes, place them in a saucepan with the butter and cook till soft. Now add the duck, the wine, herbs and seasonings. Cover and simmer for 1¼ hours, then add the papper-delle and cook gently for a further 15 minutes or until the papper-delle is soft.

CASSEROLED DUCK WITH CURAÇAO SAUCE

1 duck (4 to 4½ pounds)
2½ level tablespoons flour
1 level teaspoon celery salt
pepper
2 onions, chopped
6 ounces mushrooms
½ cup water

1 tablespoon soy sauce
3 tablespoons curaçao liqueur
seasoning
½ teaspoon dried basil
3 oranges
a little sugar

Place the flour, celery salt and a little pepper in a paper bag. Shake well, and in this seasoned flour toss the duck, cut into pieces. Shake well to coat evenly and then place the duck joints in a deep casserole. Sprinkle with the chopped onions and any flour remaining in the bag. Peel the mushrooms, slice them and add to the casserole. Mix the water, soy sauce, curaçao and one level teaspoon of salt together and pour this over the duck. Sprinkle with the dried basil, cover and bake for 1½ to 2 hours, until the joints are very tender. Cook at 325° F (Gas 3), but if the gravy is boiling too fast after the first half-hour, reduce the heat.

Meanwhile, peel and slice the oranges, place them on a flat oven-proof dish and sprinkle with the sugar. Heat through in the oven for about 10 minutes before the dish is ready, and use the orange slices to garnish the finished dish, together with a few sprigs of parsley. This quantity should make about 6 servings. You can, if you wish, substitute 4 tablespoons of fresh orange juice and 1 level tablespoon of sugar in place of the curaçao.

SALMI OF DUCK

1 duck
4 ounces button mushrooms
8 ounces larger mushrooms
1 glass port

few fresh apricots or peaches
or tinned pineapple
rings
bottled Cumberland sauce

Espagnole sauce

2 onions
1 large carrot
2 ounces lean bacon
2 ounces butter
1 heaped tablespoon flour

8 ounces tomatoes, fresh or
canned
1 glass white wine
1½ pints stock
bouquet garni (parsley, thyme,
bay leaf)

Prepare the duck for roasting, but do not stuff. Baste with hot fat and place in a hot oven, 400° F (Gas 6), allowing about 15 minutes per pound, and cook until the skin is crisp and brown but the meat still pink and underdone. Remove the bird from the oven, cool it until it can be handled, cut into serving pieces, making two pieces of each leg and cutting the breast into four.

Espagnole sauce
While the bird is cooking, make the Espagnole sauce by chopping the onions and carrot and bacon and frying them in the butter until they are rich and brown. Sprinkle in the flour, continue frying until that too has cooked to a golden brown. Now add the tomatoes, the wine and stock. Bring to the boil, stirring constantly. Finally add the bouquet garni, and simmer uncovered for an hour, stirring occasionally to prevent sticking. Strain the sauce into a clean pan, pressing the mixture in the strainer to squeeze as much liquid as possible. Simmer again for about 20 minutes, and the sauce is now ready to use.

Meanwhile, boil the button mushrooms in salted water for 5 minutes, strain and reserve for garnish. Stir the glass of port into the Espagnole sauce, reheat and add Cumberland sauce, a dessertspoon at a time, until you have got as much of an orangey flavour as you want. If you have no Cumberland sauce, then use orange juice and grated rind. Put the larger mushrooms in a casserole and on top of them the pieces of duck. Check the flavouring of the sauce and add salt and pepper if necessary, then pour the sauce over the duck, cover and cook slowly in the oven for $\frac{3}{4}$ hour or until tender. Serve on to a warm dish, garnish with the button mushrooms and the fruit (apricots, peaches or pineapple), heated through.

Cold or Left-over Duck

Duck being less fleshy than chicken in proportion to its size, there is not usually much to use up as "left-overs". However, if you have some remains from a cooked bird, you will find plenty of ideas among the Chicken Left-overs section which can be used. Similarly, many of the cold dishes and salad ideas are equally suitable for cold duck, if you want to cook your bird in advance for a cold meal.

Small Game Birds

Pheasant

Although the cock bird is more beautiful to look at, countrymen declare that the hen bird is better to eat, especially cold.

In a young bird, the first wing tip feather is pointed; in an older bird, it is rounded. If the upper part of the beak is pliable, you may be sure that you have a young bird.

An average-sized pheasant makes four servings, but before cooking it needs to be well hung, otherwise the flesh will be tasteless and dry. Hang the bird, unplucked, in a good current of air, for at least three days. In warm or muggy weather, this should be sufficient for the putrefaction process to have begun, but if the weather is cold, longer time should be allowed. It is, of course, important to keep flies away, and a thorough sprinkling of the feathers with pepper helps to do so. Individual tastes vary as to how "high" a bird should be before it is ready for cooking. Unless you wish to have a very gamey flavour, the bird will be ready for plucking when the tail feathers pull out easily. If, when you come to cook the bird, you find it has become rather too "high" for your liking, wash the bird, when plucked, in salted water to which vinegar has been added, then rinse thoroughly. Pluck, draw, truss and singe the bird, as for chicken.

ROAST PHEASANT

1 pheasant	flour
butter	seasoning
strips fat bacon	

Tie strips of fat bacon across the breast of the seasoned bird, and place a piece of butter in the cavity. Pour melted butter over the bird and roast in a pre-heated hot oven (450° F, Gas 8) for about 10 minutes, then reduce the heat to 400° F (Gas 6). Cook for about a further 45 minutes, or until tender, but baste frequently with the butter during cooking. About 15 minutes before cooking is completed, remove the bacon from the breast, dredge with flour, baste again and complete cooking. Dish the bird on to a hot platter, remove the trussing strings and serve with bread sauce, fried or oven-roasted bread-crumbs and thin gravy.

As a variation of the above, place about 4 ounces rump steak in the bird's cavity before cooking. This can be reserved and eaten cold for another meal. For this method, dripping can replace butter for roasting fat.

Here are some other recipes for roasting pheasant, giving a variety of flavourings.

FRENCH ROAST PHEASANT

1 pheasant	1 tablespoon cream cheese
2 ounces belly of pork	1 tablespoon double cream
6 walnuts, coarsely chopped	salt and pepper
2 dozen seedless grapes	butter
strips of fat bacon	

Chop the liver, mince the belly of pork. Mix together, then add the cheese, walnuts, cream and grapes. Season, and place this stuffing in the bird's cavity, stitching up the opening. Truss the bird, brush with butter, tie fat bacon strips over the breast, season, and roast at 400° F (Gas 6) for about 45 to 50 minutes or until tender. Use the remaining giblets to make a gravy.

CHESTNUT-STUFFED PHEASANT

fat bacon strips	$\frac{1}{2}$ cup chopped celery
1 pheasant	1 teaspoon salt
1 pound chestnuts	$\frac{1}{8}$ teaspoon pepper
1 cup white bread-crumbs	$\frac{1}{2}$ cup melted butter
4 chipolata sausages	2 tablespoons cream
1 tablespoon chopped parsley	

Cook, shell, skin and sieve the chestnuts, then mix with the chipolata sausages, finely chopped, the crumbs, parsley, celery, seasonings, butter and cream. Prepare the pheasant in the usual way, stuff with the above mixture, tie fat bacon pieces across the breast and roast as in previous recipe.

SAUSAGE AND LIVER-STUFFED PHEASANT

1 pheasant	1 tablespoon cream
fat bacon strips	1 glass sherry
8 ounces sausage meat	1 dessertspoon tomato
3 chicken livers	purée
1 egg yolk	nutmeg

½ teaspoon chopped parsley   butter
salt and pepper   a little stock

Mix together the sausage meat, the chicken livers (chopped) and parsley. Season with salt and pepper and bind to a stiff mixture with the beaten egg yolk and cream. Prepare the bird as usual, stuff with the mixture and tie fat bacon strips across the breast. Baste with melted butter and roast at 400° F (Gas 6) for 15 minutes. Lower the heat to 375° F (Gas 5) for 10 minutes longer, then pour into the pan the wine, tomato purée and a dash of nutmeg, together with a little stock made from the bird's giblets. Continue roasting the bird until tender, basting frequently with the sauce in the pan, and use this sauce to pour over the bird when it is ready for serving.

ITALIAN PHEASANT WITH CREAM

1 pheasant   ½ pint double cream
fat bacon strips   1 tablespoon lemon juice
2 ounces butter   salt and pepper
1 small onion

Tie the bacon strips across the breast of the seasoned pheasant, baste with melted butter and cook very slowly in a Dutch oven for about 2 hours. Remove the bacon for the last 30 minutes, pour the cream over the bird, and baste frequently. When the pheasant is dished on to a serving platter, add the lemon juice to the gravy remaining in the pan, mix well, and serve with the bird.

PHEASANT IN WINE SAUCE

1 pheasant   1 cup stock
fat bacon strips   ½ cup red wine
salt and pepper   ¼ teaspoon meat extract
2 ounces butter

Prepare and roast the pheasant as on page 145, until tender. Remove the bird to a serving dish, pour off the fat carefully from the pan, then add the wine, stock (made from bird giblets if possible) and meat extract. Bring slowly to the boil, stirring vigorously to incorporate all the goodness from the pan, then pour a little of the sauce over the bird, serving the remainder in a sauce-boat.

BRANDIED PHEASANT

1 pheasant	1 teaspoon brandy
8 ounces cooked fresh pork	1 sharp apple
1 chicken liver	salt and pepper
1 pheasant liver	2 strips fat bacon
pinch thyme	1 teaspoon Madeira
pinch rosemary	½ cup stock

Mince the pork, lean and fat, together with the chicken and pheasant livers, add thyme and rosemary, stir in the brandy and the apple, previously peeled and diced. Next add the seasoning and stuff the bird with this mixture. Truss it and tie the bacon strips over the breast. Roast in a 350° F (Gas 4) oven for about an hour or until brown and tender, basting frequently with the pan juices. When the bird is cooked, remove it to a warm serving dish. Discard the bacon. Into the roasting pan put a ½ cup of stock made from ½ teaspoon meat glaze dissolved in ½ cup hot water. Stir the pan thoroughly to incorporate all the juices from the bird and then pour the sauce into a small saucepan. Skim the fat from the surface, stir in the Madeira, reheat and serve this sauce with the bird.

DEVILLED PHEASANT

1 pheasant	salt and pepper
½ pint double cream	½ cup milk
½ teaspoon mustard	8 ounces mushrooms
½ teaspoon Worcester sauce	butter
½ teaspoon Escoffier's Sauce Diable	

Roast the pheasant in the usual manner. Meanwhile cook the mushrooms in butter in readiness for when the bird is cooked. Mix the cream, milk, mustard, sauces together and season with salt and pepper. When the bird is tender cut it into pieces, place on an earthenware dish and pour the cream sauce over it. Put it back in the oven but make sure that it does not boil. Serve with the mushrooms.

CASSEROLE OF PHEASANT WITH CHESTNUTS

1 tablespoon corn oil	grated rind and juice of ½ orange
1 pheasant	1 dessertspoon cranberry sauce
½ pound chestnuts, peeled	1 teaspoon red wine vinegar
½ pound button onions	bouquet garni

$\frac{3}{4}$ ounce cornflour

salt and pepper

1 chicken stock cube dissolved in $\frac{3}{4}$ pint of boiling water

2 tablespoons parsley, chopped

Heat the corn oil in a casserole and slowly brown the pheasant. Remove from the pan. Sauté the chestnuts and onions until browned. Remove from the pan, add the cornflour. Stir in the chicken stock, grated rind and juice from orange, cranberry sauce, red wine vinegar, bouquet garni and seasoning. Bring to the boil, stirring all the time. Add the pheasant, chestnuts and onions. Cover and cook in a slow oven, 325° F (Gas 3) for $1\frac{1}{2}$ to 2 hours. When cooked, joint the pheasant and place on a clean serving dish with the chestnuts and onions. Remove the bouquet garni from the sauce. Adjust the seasoning if necessary. Pour over the pheasant and sprinkle with chopped parsley.

CASSEROLED PHEASANT

1 pheasant

4 ounces mushrooms

1 ounce butter

1 tablespoon oil

1 orange

$\frac{1}{2}$ pint chicken stock

$\frac{1}{4}$ pint orange juice

2 wine glasses white wine

2 ounces flour

salt and pepper

Melt the oil and butter in a pan and fry the pheasant, previously plucked, drawn and jointed, on each side. When the joints are well brown, lift from the pan into an ovenproof casserole. Fry the mushrooms for a few minutes, add them to the casserole. Season. Stir the flour into the fat in the pan, cook for 2 minutes, remove from the heat, and gradually add the stock, wine and orange juice. Bring to the boil, stirring, and when it thickens pour it into the casserole. Place the dish in the middle of the oven and cook until the pheasant is tender. Skin the orange, remove the pith so that only the outer skin remains, and cut this into thin strips. Simmer the orange strips in water until soft, then when the casserole is ready, sprinkle them over the bird portions, and garnish with orange segments.

GRILLED PHEASANT

1 pheasant

2 ounces butter

salt and pepper

1 egg

bread-crumbs

4 ounces mushrooms

2 tomatoes

watercress

Melt the butter in a pan and in it place the bird, jointed, and season. Fry until the pieces are lightly browned, then remove from the pan and press them between two plates until quite cold. Next coat the pieces with egg and bread-crumbs, place under a grill for a few minutes until the coating has set, then brush with melted butter and cook, turning frequently, for about 25 to 30 minutes. Serve, garnished with grilled mushrooms, tomatoes and sprigs of watercress.

BRAISED PHEASANT

1 pheasant	1 small onion
1 thin slice salt pork	2 teaspoons flour
1 tangerine	$\frac{1}{4}$ cup Madeira
2 tablespoons lard or cooking fat	$\frac{1}{2}$ teaspoon salt
1 dozen mushrooms	a little freshly-ground pepper
2 tablespoons butter	1 sprig fresh fennel (optional)

Prepare the pheasant for cooking, pre-heat the oven to 400° F (Gas 6). Flatten the slice of pork and insert it under the skin of the breast flesh. Into the body cavity place the pheasant's liver and the tangerine (peeled), then close the cavity by stitching tightly. Truss the pheasant and brown it in the lard melted in a heavy pan. Baste and turn frequently until the bird is golden all over and then transfer it to a casserole. In the fat fry the mushrooms, using the caps only, for a few moments, and then place them over the pheasant in the casserole. In a saucepan melt the butter and in it cook the onion, minced or very finely chopped, and the flour. Cook but do not allow this onion to brown. When soft, gradually stir in the Madeira, salt and pepper and pour the sauce over the bird. Add a sprig of fennel if available, then cover the casserole and cook for 30 to 40 minutes until the pheasant is tender.

Guinea Fowl

Guinea fowl has grey plumage with white spots and is generally a little larger than pheasant. Although available all the year round, they are at their prime best from February to June. Choose a bird with a plump breast and smooth-skinned feet, but be sure not to cook it too soon after it has been killed.

A guinea fowl is prepared in exactly the same way as chicken and may be cooked similarly too, especially casseroling and stewing. However, this bird lacks fat so it is important to make sure that, when roasting, the flesh does not dry out in cooking. It should be covered with bacon strips or fat bacon and basted frequently or, alternatively, wrapped in aluminium foil.

ROAST GUINEA FOWL

1 guinea fowl	2 ounces butter
2 to 4 slices fat bacon	salt and pepper

Beat the salt and pepper into the butter and place it in the cavity of the prepared bird. Truss. Lay the slices of bacon over the breast and place in a baking tin. Baste with a little melted butter. Roast in a fairly hot oven, 375° F (Gas 5), for 1 to 1½ hours depending on size. Baste frequently. When the bird is almost ready, dredge the breast with flour, baste again and finish cooking. Serve with browned crumbs and bread sauce.

ROAST GUINEA FOWL WITH GRAPES

1 guinea fowl	2 tablespoons flour
3 ounces softened butter	½ pound green grapes
sprig parsley	½ glass sherry
4 to 5 rashers fat bacon	bouquet garni
giblet stock	pepper and salt

Make some stock with water, the giblets and the bouquet garni. Season with a little pepper and salt. Put half butter and parsley sprig inside the bird cavity. Spread the remaining butter thickly over the bird and cover the breast with the bacon. Roast in a pre-heated oven at 400° F (Gas 6) until golden brown and tender (about an hour). Baste frequently during this cooking time.

When the bird is cooked, remove it to a serving dish. Pour the fat carefully off the roasting tin leaving just a thin layer on the bottom. To this add sufficient flour to absorb the fat. Stirring continuously and scraping all the residue from the bottom of the pan, fry over the heat to make a roux. When this has become a good colour, stir in about ¼ pint giblet stock and add the sherry. Now add the green grapes, previously skinned and seeded, and cook this sauce gently for about 10 minutes. Test for seasoning. Add salt and pepper and, if liked, a squeeze of lemon juice. Strain the gravy into a previously heated sauce-boat and garnish the serving-dish with the grapes.

BRAISED GUINEA HEN À L'ORANGE

1 guinea fowl	salt and pepper
2 tablespoons butter	2 bouquets garnis
½ carrot	stock
1 medium onion	1 teaspoon cornflour
1 tablespoon diced bacon	orange liqueur (orange curaçao)

Make stock from the wing tips, neck and giblets of the bird, together with one slice taken from the onion, one of the bouquets garnis, salt and pepper. Melt one tablespoon of the butter in a heavy pan, and in this brown the prepared and trussed guinea hen on all sides. Meanwhile, in a casserole big enough to take the bird, melt the other tablespoon of butter and in it sauté slowly the half carrot, sliced, and the remainder of the onion, chopped, together with the diced bacon. Add salt, pepper and the remaining bouquet garni.

When the vegetables are lightly browned, place the guinea hen in the casserole and over it pour 2 tablespoons of the orange liqueur. Set it aflame and when the flames have died, add one cup of hot stock. Cover the casserole, and cook the bird at 350° F (Gas 4) for about an hour or until tender. For the last 10 minutes of cooking time, remove the lid in order to brown the bird. When done, place it on a hot serving dish and keep it warm. Skim the fat from the juices, strain them through a fine sieve. Force the vegetables through the sieve, or blend in an electric blender. Dissolve the cornflour in a little cold stock, add to the gravy and sieved vegetables and reheat, stirring until the sauce thickens. When cooked, stir in 2 teaspoons of the orange liqueur. Cut the bird into 4 portions. Garnish with a little minced parsley and hand the sauce separately in a hot sauce-boat.

Grouse

In season 12 August to 10 December
A young bird will have soft downy feathers on its breast, and when you hold it by the lower mandible between your finger and thumb, moving it gently up and down, the mandible should bend or break. Older

grouse are perfectly usable but they should be casseroled and not roasted or grilled.

Hang the birds by their legs for at least three days, preferably five or six, according to the weather. Then pluck and draw them as for pheasant. The plucking is a more delicate operation than with pheasant and should be done with the greatest possible care so as not to tear the skin.

ROAST GROUSE

1 or more birds

For each bird

1 ounce butter *or* 4 ounces rump steak	1 rasher bacon
	flour
salt and pepper	1 slice toast

Into each bird insert either 1 ounce butter or a piece of rump steak seasoned with salt and pepper. (The steak can be used for a cold meat and salad dish on another occasion.) Cover the breast of the bird with bacon and roast at 375° F to 400° F (Gas 5–6) until tender (about 30 minutes) in the centre of the oven. Baste frequently. When the bird has been cooking for about 20 minutes remove the bacon, dredge the breast with flour and return it to the oven on a slice of toast. During the rest of the cooking time, the bread will absorb the liquid which drips from the bird. Serve on the toast on which it was roasted with bread sauce, fried or oven-baked crumbs and thin gravy.

CASSEROLED GROUSE

1 grouse (or more)	freshly-ground black pepper
2 tablespoons flour	dry draught cider
2 tablespoons olive oil	pinch of thyme
1 ounce butter	1 clove garlic
1 onion	4 ounces mushrooms

Using a knife and shears, cut the birds in half lengthwise. Place the onion, finely sliced, in a large bowl. Place on it the pieces of grouse, the pepper, some salt and cover with the cider. Leave the grouse to marinate overnight.

Next day, lift the grouse from the marinade, dry each piece, roll it in flour and fry in the olive oil and butter, mixed and melted in a casserole just large enough to take the bird or birds. Pour the marinade into the casserole, add the garlic, finely chopped, the mushrooms, whole, a pinch of pepper and a sprinkling of thyme. If the bird or birds are still not covered, add sufficient water, then place the casserole in the oven, bring it to the boil, and then simmer until the meat leaves the bones easily (1¼ hours approximately). Serve with usual vegetables.

GRILLED GROUSE

1 grouse	cooking oil

For this the bird must be young. Split it down the back and flatten the breast. Brush with cooking oil and place under the grill, bony side towards the heat. Grill for about 7 minutes, then turn and grill for the same length of time on the other side. Serve with bread sauce.
Note Only the breast of the bird is used.

BANANA-STUFFED GROUSE

1 or more grouse	1 level teaspoon salt
2 bananas per bird	10 drops lemon juice
1 level teaspoon black pepper	

Skin the bananas, mash them and mix with the pepper, salt and lemon juice. Stuff this mixture into the grouse cavity and roast in the usual way (see page 153).

CASSEROLED GROUSE AND SAUSAGE

2 grouse	1 small white cabbage
4 rashers streaky bacon	4 fluid ounces dry red wine
4 dessertspoons flour	½ pint stock
2 ounces butter or lard	4 smoked sausages
1 onion	black pepper
4 ounces pickled belly of pork	salt

This recipe is excellent for older birds and makes a succulent meal.

Trim the rind and gristle from the bacon, and cover the breasts of the prepared birds. Truss them and roll in the flour, shaking off any surplus. Melt the butter or lard in a pan and in it brown the birds all over. Remove them from the pan, and in the remaining fat fry the onion (sliced) and the pickled pork (diced) until it is just lightly brown in colour.

Meanwhile shred the cabbage, discarding the stalk, and cook it for 5 minutes in boiling, salted water. Drain and put half the cabbage in the bottom of a casserole and add to it the fried pork and onion.

Place the birds on top, pack in the remaining cabbage, season with pepper, then pour in the wine and stock, cover and cook either over a low heat on top of the stove, or in a moderate oven 325° F (Gas 3) for about 1½ hours or until tender. After the casserole has been cooking for about 45 minutes, add the smoked sausages, and put in a little extra liquid if required. Serve with boiled or baked potatoes. Do not use very much salt to season because the sausages are in themselves rather salty.

GROUSE PUDDING

1 grouse
1 pound stewing steak
1 ounce flour
½ pint stock
8 ounces plain flour

4 ounces suet
1 teaspoon baking powder
cold water
salt and pepper

First make the suet pastry. If using butcher's suet, chop it finely with a little flour; sift the flour, salt and baking powder together, mix in the suet and add enough cold water to make a firm dough.

Cut the steak and the flesh from the bird into small pieces and dip them in seasoned flour. Line a greased basin with two-thirds of your suet pastry, put into it the meat and half the stock. Make a lid with the remaining pastry, cover the basin and make a hole in the centre. Cover with a grease-proof paper and steam for 4 or more hours, pouring in the remaining stock, previously heated, at the half time mark.

An old bird can be used for this recipe. It will depend on the age and toughness of the bird as to how long you leave it to cook. You can if you wish add a sliced onion or a few mushrooms to the contents of the pudding.

BRAISED GROUSE

1 brace grouse
2 carrots, sliced
2 onions, sliced
1 small turnip, sliced
bouquet garni
1 chicken stock cube
¾ pint boiling water

1 tablespoon cornflour
1 tablespoon sherry
½ teaspoon soy sauce
1 tablespoon jellied cranberry
    sauce
seasoning

Prepare the grouse as for roasting. Place vegetables in the base of the casserole with bouquet garni. Dissolve the stock cube in boiling water. Put grouse on top and pour over the stock. Cover and cook in an oven at 350° F (Gas 4) for 1½ hours, basting occasionally with the stock. Remove the lid for the last ½ hour to brown the birds. Remove to a hot serving dish, strain the liquid from casserole and arrange the vegetables around the birds. Blend the stock with the cornflour. Pour into a pan and bring to the boil, stirring. Add sherry, soy sauce, cranberry jelly and seasoning to taste. Reheat and pour over the grouse.

GROUSE PIE

Whole roast grouse can be bought in large cans and this used with pork fillet can make a large, party-sized pie, sufficient for eight or more servings.

1 can whole roast grouse	salt and pepper
¾ pound pork fillet	

For the pastry

1½ pounds plain flour	2 level teaspoons salt
7½ ounces English lard	a little beaten egg for glazing
1¾ gills water	3 hard-boiled eggs

To make this pie you will need a raised pie mould, about 8 inches long and 3½ inches wide at the maximum. Open the tin of grouse, heat it to melt the jelly, remove all the bones, and set the jelly on one side for use next day. Cut the pork fillets into one inch cubes and dust lightly with salt and pepper. Shell the hard-boiled eggs.

To make the pastry, sift the flour and salt into a bowl, put the lard and water into a saucepan, melt the lard over a low heat, bring it to the boil, and then pour it immediately into the flour, mixing with a knife. Knead the dough by hand until it is quite smooth. Cut off a quarter of the pastry for the lid and set on one side in a warm place. Clip the halves of the pie mould together and stand on a baking tray. Put the large piece of pastry into the mould and work it up the sides with your fingers to ¼ inch above the top. Now put half the pork into the bottom of the pie, then the hard-boiled eggs, laying lengthways down the pie, and then cover with the grouse. Finally add the rest of the pork.

Form the remaining pastry into an oval, large enough to fit the top of the pie. Damp the edges of the pastry above the mould, place the lid in position, and press well into the pastry beneath. Trim the edges and set the trimmings aside in a warm place, for use as decoration. Crimp the pie edges and brush the surface with beaten egg. Make a large hole in the centre of the pie to allow steam to escape. Roll out the pastry scraps, cut diamond shapes for leaves and lay them round the hole.

Cut a strip about 1 inch wide, fringe it along one edge with cuts about ¼ inch apart and roll it up to form a tassel. Place it carefully around the centre of the hole, but be careful not to block it. Brush this decoration with beaten egg.

Pre-heat your oven to 400° F (Gas 6) and place the pie in the centre of the oven. Bake for 30 minutes then reduce the heat to 350° F (Gas 4) for a further half hour. Now cover the pie with grease-proof paper and reduce the heat to 325° F (Gas 3) for a further hour. When the pie is cooked, take it from the oven, but leave it on the tray inside the mould until the following day.

Next day, heat the pie very slightly in order to loosen the mould, unclip it and remove. Melt the jellied stock from the grouse, cool it but do not allow it to set again. Now insert the tip of a funnel into the hole in the pie centre, and carefully pour in the liquid stock to fill the pie. Leave to cool so that the jelly sets. When the pie is thoroughly cold, serve it with salad.

POTTED GROUSE

1 bird (or more)	cayenne
butter or stock	clarified butter
salt and pepper	

Roast the grouse if young, or casserole if old. Cool, then remove the skin and bones from the bird, and mince or chop the meat very finely. Pound the meat until it is quite smooth, and gradually add game stock or oiled butter, until the mixture is soft and moist. Season well with salt and pepper and a dash of cayenne, and press the mixture into small pots. Cover with clarified butter and use as required as a spread on biscuits or bread or in pastry cases.

Partridge

In season 1 September to 1 February
The best bird for the table is considered to be the grey partridge, and you can distinguish a young bird from an old one by the fact that its long wing feather is pointed. In older birds this wing feather is rounded. Its beak will be yellow and its legs dark. Older birds must be braised,

casseroled or marinated, even if they have been hung for a number of days. Partridges should be plucked, singed, cleaned and trussed as for pheasant.

ROAST PARTRIDGE

1 young partridge per person salt and pepper
1 rasher fat bacon per bird   1 slice bread per bird
butter

Put a large piece of butter into the cavity of each prepared bird. Season well, and then tie a rasher of fat bacon over each breast. Place the birds in a baking tin in hot butter and roast them in a medium-to-hot oven for about 20 minutes. 5 minutes before the cooking time is up, remove the bacon so that the breasts brown.

Meanwhile, fry the slices of bread in butter, removing the crusts, and shaping the bread to make a cushion to receive the partridges. Place each partridge on one of the croûtons, then pour over them the butter and other juices from the roasting pan. Serve with bread sauce, and fried or oven-baked bread-crumbs and garnish with watercress.

PARTRIDGE IN VINE LEAVES

A well-known way of cooking partridges of any age is wrapped in vine leaves. These can be obtained in tins or in brine from many specialist delicatessen shops.

1 partridge per person   salt and pepper
flour   vine leaves
butter

Season the prepared partridges and place them in the butter melted in a pan. Brown the birds all over, then remove them from the pan and wrap each one in large vine leaves. Tie round with fine string to hold in place. Now put the birds in a casserole, pour over the melted butter, sprinkle with flour, add a little more seasoning, then cover closely and cook in a moderate oven, 350° F (Gas 4), for about an hour or until the birds are tender, which will depend on their age.

VINE LEAF WRAPPED PARTRIDGES IN WINE

1 partridge per person   stock
vine leaves   wine
salt and pepper

Wrap each seasoned partridge in vine leaves and place the birds in a casserole. Almost cover with a mixture half wine, half stock, and simmer for 35 minutes. Lift the birds from the casserole, place in a baking tin, baste with melted butter and roast for a further 25 minutes. Remove the vine leaves towards the end of the cooking, say for the last 5 minutes or so, to allow the breasts to brown. Make a gravy from the pan juices and the stock, and pour over the birds when serving with new potatoes and watercress.

FRENCH PARTRIDGES ON THE SPIT

1 partridge per person	walnut meats
salt and pepper	1 slice bacon per bird
black olives	1 slice fried bread per bird

Season the cavities of the prepared birds, from which the feet have been removed, with salt and pepper. Place two or three black olives inside, together with a few broken walnut meats. Wrap the birds in bacon, tie them with fine string, and skewer them on to a long spit, roasting over a good bed of glowing coals, and turning often. The birds can be cooked on a rotating electric spit. When the birds are cooked, remove the wrappings and serve each bird on a slice of bread previously fried in butter.

STEWED PARTRIDGE

2 partridges	$\frac{1}{4}$ pint port wine
1 ounce butter	$\frac{1}{4}$ pint white stock
2 tablespoons flour	salt and pepper

Dredge the birds inside and out with the seasonings. Melt the butter in a shallow pan, and in it fry the birds, turning occasionally, until they are evenly brown. Lift the birds on to a plate and add the flour to the butter in the pan, stirring until it becomes pale gold in colour. Now add the stock and wine, and when it is smooth and has reached boiling point, return the birds to the pan and cover closely. Simmer gently for about $1\frac{3}{4}$ hours. Serve garnished with watercress and accompanied by the gravy from the sauce-boat. Quite elderly birds will make a very nice meal when cooked in this manner.

FRIED PARTRIDGES

2 partridges	1 tablespoon chopped parsley
$\frac{1}{2}$ pint olive oil	browned bread-crumbs
1 bay leaf	salt and pepper

Using young partridges, cut them in two lengthwise, and flatten with a rolling pin. Make a marinade of the oil, salt, pepper, parsley and the bay leaf, dried and crushed. Place the pieces of bird in this marinade for an hour or longer if possible. Then lift the pieces from the oil, drain slightly, and then rub each in the browned bread-crumbs. Fry each piece on both sides in hot oil until the flesh is tender. As each portion of bird is ready, keep it warm on a serving-dish until the rest of the cooking has been completed.

PARTRIDGE WITH CABBAGE

2 partridges
1 medium-sized cabbage
4 ounces bacon
1 onion
lard or margarine

bouquet garni
stock (about 1 pint)
nutmeg
sausages (optional)
salt and pepper

This is another recipe suitable for birds past their first youth. Cut the cabbage in quarters. Take off the outer leaves and the hardest part of the stalk, wash well and cook in boiling salted water for a few minutes. Drain well. Split the partridges in half and fry in the fat until golden brown and crisp. Line the casserole with the bacon slices, then put on top half the cabbage, season with salt and pepper, sprinkle with a little nutmeg, then put in the onion, thinly sliced, and on top of this the pieces of fried partridge. Now add the rest of the cabbage together with a little more seasoning, then almost cover with stock. Place the casserole lid in position and cook in the middle of the oven for about 1½ to 2 hours, adding a little more stock if necessary. Three or four chipolata sausages or 2 smoked sausages may if required be added to the casserole, or, if preferred, may be fried separately, and used as a garnish to the finished dish. Serve the pieces of bird on a bed of shredded cabbage. This quantity is sufficient for 4 servings.

Pigeon

Pigeons are available all the year round, but it is important, especially for roast pigeon, that the birds should be young, with pinkish legs and claws, well-covered limbs and breasts and skin which is not dark in colour. Young birds are, of course, smaller in size and their beaks look disproportionately large. They will not have grown the white neck ring. In an older bird the feet and legs are of a bright coral colour.

Pigeon is easy to pluck because the feathers are loose and the skin tough. Plucking, drawing and trussing are done in the same way as for other birds. Leave the feet on because it makes for simplicity in trussing and tying the legs together. Pigeon is liable to be dry, so that more fat bacon than usual should be used when roasting. Pigeon does not need hanging for more than a couple of days after shooting. Keep them in a cool, airy place, protected, of course, from flies.

Older birds, when cooked whole, have a tendency to impart a slightly bitter flavour to a dish. This derives from the back-bone, and it is therefore advisable when cooking a bird which has passed its youth to halve it and remove this back-bone.

ROAST PIGEON

2 young pigeons	2 slices fried bread or toast
2 ounces butter	salt and pepper
2 rashers fat bacon	a little lemon juice

Mix the butter with the lemon juice and put half in each bird cavity, the birds having of course been previously prepared for roasting. Truss, cover each with fat bacon, tied in place, and roast in a fairly hot oven, 375 to 400° F (Gas 5–6), for about 30 minutes. Baste once or twice during this cooking time. Just before the bird is cooked, remove the bacon and allow it to brown for about 10 minutes. You can, if you wish, put the fried bread or toast under the birds at this stage for the final 10 minutes of cooking. Otherwise place the birds on the bread when the cooking is complete. Garnish with watercress and serve with gravy and bread sauce.

PIGEONS WITH GREEN PEAS

2 young pigeons	2 tablespoons whole berry
4 tablespoons corn oil	cranberry sauce
8 to 10 small white onions,	$\frac{1}{2}$ pint chicken stock
peeled	$\frac{1}{2}$ pound fresh green peas
4 ounces bacon diced	bouquet garni
1 tablespoon cornflour	salt, pepper

Clean and truss as for roasting. Heat the corn oil in a casserole and sauté the pigeons until evenly browned. Remove the pigeons, add the onions and bacon and sauté until golden. Add the cornflour, stir in the chicken stock and cranberry sauce. Bring to the boil, stirring all the time. Add the pigeons, green peas and bouquet garni. Season to taste, cover and cook in a slow oven, 300° F (Gas 2) for $1\frac{1}{4}$ to $1\frac{1}{2}$ hours.

CASSEROLED PIGEON

2 young pigeons

3 ounces bacon

1 medium onion

1 ounce butter

$\frac{3}{4}$ pint stock

1 carrot

1 ounce flour

bouquet garni

salt and pepper

Prepare and truss the pigeons as for roasting. Melt the butter in a pan and in it fry the pigeons, bacon and onion until all are well browned. Transfer to a casserole, pour over the stock, add the bouquet garni and the vegetables, diced, cover and simmer until the birds are tender, about 1 to $1\frac{1}{2}$ hours. Blend the flour into a little cold stock or water and add this to the casserole. Bring back to boiling point, stir, re-cover and simmer for a further 10 minutes. When the birds are cooked, lift from the casserole, cut off the trussing strings and split the birds in half. Place them on a hot serving-dish. Skim excess fat from the sauce and pour over the pieces of bird.

PIGEONS IN BEER

2 pigeons

1 medium onion

2 bay leaves

salt and pepper

draught beer (mild or bitter)

flour

olive oil

1 beaten egg yolk

Soak the pigeons' livers overnight in a marinade of draught beer, sliced raw onion, salt, pepper and bay leaves. Next day remove the livers from the marinade, dry, flour and fry them in a little olive oil. Split the birds in half, remove the back-bone and place the pieces together with the livers into a casserole. Pour over the marinade and add further beer (or, if you prefer, water) to cover the flesh. Simmer in the oven for about 1 to $1\frac{1}{4}$ hours until the meat lifts away from the bone without difficulty. Place the pieces of bird on a warm serving dish, strain the gravy into a small saucepan and stir in a beaten egg yolk to thicken, first of course removing the saucepan from the heat. Pour this sauce over the birds before serving.

PIGEON PUDDING

2 pigeons
6 ounces rump steak
1 tablespoon flour

2 hard-boiled eggs
salt and pepper
$\frac{1}{2}$ cup stock

For the pastry

10 ounces flour
5 ounces suet
pinch salt

level teaspoon baking powder
pinch mixed herbs
cold water

If using butcher's suet, chop it finely with flour. Make suet pastry, by sifting the flour, salt and baking powder together, and mixing in the suet and herbs. Add sufficient cold water to make a firm dough. Roll out the pastry, reserving a piece for the pudding lid and using the rest to line a basin. Remove the feet from the pigeons, then split the birds in half and remove the skin. Cut the steak into small cubes and dip both pigeon pieces and steak into seasoned flour. Cut the hard-boiled eggs into quarters. Into a lined basin put the prepared birds, steak and egg. Add the stock, cover with a lid made from the remaining pastry, and steam for 3 to $3\frac{1}{2}$ hours. Meanwhile make some extra stock or gravy to serve with the pudding when ready.

GRILLED PIGEON

2 pigeons
salt and pepper

2 ounces butter
slices of toast

Split the prepared birds down the back, flatten and cut away the back-bone. Brush the pieces all over with oiled butter or cooking oil, season with salt and pepper and place under a pre-heated grill. Cook for about 20 minutes, turning occasionally. Serve on slices of toast or fried bread, and pour over the drippings from the grill pan.

PIGEON PIE

2 pigeons
2 ounces butter or margarine
8 ounces bacon
1 onion
2 tomatoes

1 dessertspoon flour
$\frac{3}{4}$ pint stock
$\frac{1}{2}$ teaspoon meat extract
salt and pepper

For the pastry

8 ounces plain flour
1 teaspoon baking powder
pinch of salt

3 ounces lard
$\frac{1}{2}$ ounce margarine
cold water

Cook the pigeons in advance, before you want to use the pie at a meal. Heat the butter or margarine in a pan and in it fry the pigeons, halved lengthways and with back-bones removed, until they are well browned. Lift from the fat and place the pieces in a deep casserole. In the remaining fat fry the bacon until lightly brown, then sprinkle the bacon over the pigeons.

Fry the onion until brown and leave in the pan. Add the tomatoes, cook a further 5 minutes then sprinkle in the flour and stir over the heat, cooking for a further minute or two. Now add the stock, bring to the boil, stirring continuously, and boil for 3 minutes. Add the meat extract, seasoning and pour over the pigeons. Cover the casserole and cook in the middle of a moderate oven, pre-heated at 350° F (Gas 4) for about $1\frac{1}{2}$ hours. Leave to cool.

Next day (or later the same day) make the pastry, by sifting together the salt and flour, rubbing in the fat, adding the baking powder, and mixing with a knife to a stiff dough with cold water. Roll out the pastry, brush the rim of the casserole with water and cut a strip of pastry to fit. Pile the pieces of pigeon up to the centre of the dish, moisten the pastry rim with water lightly, and then put in place the pastry lid, pressing firmly with the thumb all round the rim. Make a hole in the centre for the steam to escape. Trim with a few diamond-shaped leaves, made from rolled-out scraps of pastry, and brush round the hole at the top and place the leaves in position. Brush the top of the pie with milk or beaten egg, and bake in a pre-heated oven 400° F (Gas 6) on the second shelf from the top for about 30 to 35 minutes.

PIGEONS ITALIAN STYLE

2 pigeons	$\frac{1}{2}$ cup wine
2 ounces butter	a little rosemary and sage
3 tablespoons oil	1 small red pepper
$\frac{1}{2}$ onion	8 ounce tin tomatoes (peeled)
2 ounces bacon	salt and pepper

Cut the prepared pigeons into serving pieces, removing back-bone. Heat the butter and oil together in a large, stout pan, and in this brown the pigeon pieces, the onion and bacon. (The onion should be thinly sliced.) Then add the wine and herbs, the pepper, seeded and chopped, and salt and pepper to taste. Cook until the wine has evaporated, then add the tomatoes, and continue to cook over a moderate heat for a further 20 to 25 minutes, or until the pigeon pieces are quite tender.

Snipe

In season 12 August to 31 January
Snipe can be eaten hung or unhung, according to personal taste. The birds should be plucked, but not drawn. Pluck not only the body but the head. Leave the head in position, but take the skin off and remove the eyes. Wipe each bird, twist the head round and, using the beak as a skewer, pass it through the legs and into the body.

Allow one bird per person as a general rule, or half a bird each, depending on size. Brush each bird over with warmed butter, then tie a thin slice of bacon over each breast and place on a slice of toast in a baking tin. Cook in a moderate oven, 350° F (Gas 4), for 15 to 20 minutes, basting frequently with the melted butter. The drippings from the trail will be caught up into the toast. Dish the birds on this toast, garnish and serve with gravy in a separate sauce-boat. Serve with fried bread-crumbs and game chips, or a salad if preferred.

Woodcock

In season 1 September to 31 January (Scotland) and 1 October to 31 January (England)
Woodcock tends to be a little rubbery if eaten too fresh. It is therefore advisable to hang it for a day or two. Prepare and cook in exactly the same way as for Snipe above.

Plover

In season 1 September to 31 January
Only two kinds of plover are allowed to be shot in Britain—the
Golden Plover and the Grey Plover. Other varieties are protected by
the Protection of Birds Act (1954).

Prepare the birds and cook them as for snipe and woodcock on p. 165.

Metric Conversion Tables

LINEAR MEASUREMENTS
(for pots, pans, cake tins, etc.)

1 metre = 100 centimetres (cm.) = $39\frac{1}{2}$ inches (approx.)

CENTIMETRES INTO INCHES (APPROX.)

cm.	in.	cm.	in.
10	4	22	$8\frac{3}{4}$
12	$4\frac{3}{4}$	24	$9\frac{1}{2}$
14	$5\frac{1}{2}$	26	$10\frac{1}{4}$
16	$6\frac{1}{4}$	28	11
18	7	30	$11\frac{3}{4}$
20	$7\frac{3}{4}$	32	$12\frac{1}{2}$

INCHES INTO CENTIMETRES (APPROX.)

in.	cm.	in.	cm.
5	13	9	23
6	15	10	25
7	18	11	28
8	20	12	30

TEMPERATURES

100 degrees Centigrade (boiling point) = 212 degrees Fahrenheit

0 degrees Centigrade (freezing point) = 32 degrees Fahrenheit

CENTIGRADE (C.) INTO FAHRENHEIT (F.)

deg. C.	deg. F.	deg. C.	deg. F.
120	248	200	392
130	266	210	410
140	284	220	428
150	302	230	446
160	320	240	464
170	338	250	482
180	356	260	500
190	374		

FAHRENHEIT INTO CENTIGRADE

deg. F.	deg. C.	deg. F.	deg. C.
250	121	400	205
275	135	425	219
300	149	450	233
325	163	475	246
350	177	500	260
375	191		

SOLIDS

1 kilogramme (kg.) = 1,000 grammes (gm.) = 2 lb. $3\frac{1}{4}$ oz. (approx.)

GRAMMES INTO OUNCES (APPROX.)

gm.	oz.	gm.	oz.
50	$1\frac{3}{4}$	300	$10\frac{1}{2}$
100	$3\frac{1}{2}$	350	$12\frac{1}{2}$
150	$5\frac{1}{4}$	400	14
200	7	450	16
250	9	500	$17\frac{1}{2}$

OUNCES INTO GRAMMES (APPROX.)

oz.	gm.	oz.	gm.
1	28	9	255
2	57	10	283
3	85	11	312
4 ($\frac{1}{4}$ lb.)	113	12 ($\frac{3}{4}$ lb.)	340
5	141	13	368
6	170	14	397
7	198	15	426
8 ($\frac{1}{2}$ lb.)	227	16 (1 lb.)	454

LIQUIDS

1 litre = 1,000 millilitres (ml.) = $1\frac{3}{4}$ pints (approx.)

MILLILITRES INTO FLUID OUNCES (APPROX.)

ml.	fl. oz.	ml.	fl. oz.
25	1	300	$10\frac{1}{2}$
50	$1\frac{3}{4}$	350	$12\frac{1}{4}$
100	$3\frac{1}{2}$	400	14
150	$5\frac{1}{4}$	450	$15\frac{3}{4}$
200	7	500 ($\frac{1}{2}$ litre)	$17\frac{1}{2}$
250 ($\frac{1}{4}$ litre)	$8\frac{3}{4}$		

FLUID OUNCES INTO MILLILITRES (APPROX.)

fl. oz.	ml.	fl. oz.	ml.
1	28	11	312
2	57	12	341
3	85	13	369
4	114	14	398
5 ($\frac{1}{4}$ pint)	142	15 ($\frac{3}{4}$ pint)	426
6	170	16	454
7	199	17	483
8	228	18	511
9	256	19	540
10 ($\frac{1}{2}$ pint)	284	20 (1 pint)	568

Index